INFORMATION, CORPORATE GOVERNANCE, AND INSTITUTIONAL DIVERSITY

Information,
Corporate Governance, and
Institutional Diversity

*Competitiveness in Japan, the USA,
and the Transitional Economies*

Masahiko Aoki

Translated by Stacey Jehlik

*This publication was supported by a generous
donation from The Daido Life Foundation*

OXFORD
UNIVERSITY PRESS

OXFORD
UNIVERSITY PRESS

Great Clarendon Street, Oxford OX2 6DP

Oxford University Press is a department of the University of Oxford.
It furthers the University's objective of excellence in research, scholarship,
and education by publishing worldwide in

Oxford New York

Athens Auckland Bangkok Bogotá Buenos Aires Calcutta
Cape Town Chennai Dar es Salaam Delhi Florence Hong Kong Istanbul
Karachi Kuala Lumpur Madrid Melbourne Mexico City Mumbai
Nairobi Paris São Paulo Shanghai Singapore Taipei Tokyo Toronto Warsaw

and associated companies in Berlin Ibadan

Oxford is a registered trade mark of Oxford University Press
in the UK and certain other countries

Published in the United States
by Oxford University Press Inc., New York

Original Japanese edition published by TOYO KEIZAI SHINPO SHA, Tokyo

English translation rights arranged with TOYO KEIZAI SHINPO SHA, Tokyo
through Tuttle-Mori Agency, Inc., Tokyo

First published in English 2000

British Library Cataloguing in Publication Data

Data available

Library of Congress Cataloging in Publication Data

Aoki, Masahiko, 1938–
Information, corporate governance, and institutional diversity: competitiveness in Japan,
the USA, and the transitional economies / Masahiko Aoki; translated by Stacey Jehlik.
p. cm.
Includes bibliographical references and index.
1. Institutional economics. 2. Knowledge management. 3. Competition. I. Title.
HB99.5 .A6 2000 658.4'038–dc21 00-034010

ISBN 0–19–829703–3

1 3 5 7 9 10 8 6 4 2

Typeset by Best-set Typesetter Ltd., Hong Kong
Printed in Great Britain
on acid-free paper by
T.J. International Ltd.,
Padstow, Cornwall

Contents

Preface to the English Edition, 2000

This book is an English translation of *Keizai Sisutemu no Shinka to Tagenesei* (The Evolution and Diversity of Economic Systems), published in Japanese in 1995 by Toyo Keizai Shinpo Sha in Tokyo. I wrote it in the fall of 1994 based on materials for an undergraduate course at the University of Tokyo which I taught as a visiting professor. The book was well received in Japan and immediately I had inquiries about the possibility of an English translation. However, at that time I was planning to write an English version of the book by myself so I declined those inquiries. I expected that, having written the Japanese version, this project would not take too much time and effort to complete. However, as soon as I started to work on it, it became immediately clear that my expectations were unrealizable. For the English version, I wanted to lay down a more rigorous game-theoretic framework for comparative institutional analysis as well as provide more extensive comparative materials beyond the comparison of Japan and the USA. As of January 2000, I finally began to feel that the project was close to completion, but the two books now are different in focus and accessibility.

Between the years 1994 and 2000, there have been many important political and economic events in Japan, as well as in East Asia and beyond. My thoughts on economics and economic systems have naturally evolved accordingly. World views on the Japanese economy have undergone a tremendous change during this period as well. However, in my opinion and judgment, no satisfactory economic treatise in English on the Japanese economy has appeared to explain the source and nature of the "crisis" in the late 1990s and suggest possible ways out of the muddle in a good comparative perspective. A conventional view in the West triumphantly asserts the end of the East Asian model (although it is not usually a well defined concept) and the need for Japan and other East Asian economies to emulate the more transparent rules of the Anglo-American model. But is this possible and desirable?

At the same time, I detect a great deal of interest emerging in Europe regarding whether or not the continental European economies will sustain their distinct institutional features in spite of the globalization of financial markets and the ongoing information and communications technology revolution as well as the creation of de facto federalist states by the unification of the currency. I am more and more convinced that mutual understanding of the historically unique paths of the various economies using common analytical tools – the theme expressed in the Foreword of the 1995 Japanese edition – is a necessity for engagement in this kind of discourse.

In 1997 I accepted the part-time position of director general of the Research Institute of the Ministry of International Trade and Industry (MITI/RI), and since then I have been commuting between Silicon Valley, where unprecedented prosperity is strikingly visible, and Kasumigaseki, where many government bureaucrats at the once-notorious MITI are earnestly working towards a reform of the Japanese economy. Looking at the workings of both systems from the inside, I am persuaded that the translation of this book even at this time is worthwhile, given the time currently available to me and the absence of comparable literature in English. I have to admit that my diagnosis of the ailing Japanese financial sector at the initial time of writing was somewhat over-kind and did not predict the magnitude of the crisis that hit the Japanese financial sector between 1997 and 1998. Yet I would like to say that my diagnosis of an information systemic source of the problem in Japan remains fundamental and relevant for understanding the revolutionary nature of the Silicon Valley phenomena. Also, the policy recommendations I advocated in Chapters 6 and 7 had a considerable impact on public debates about ongoing economic reforms in China as well as Japan.

Thus, instead of modifying the Japanese version marginally, I decided to have it translated into English exactly as it appeared in 1995 except for adding detailed references as footnotes. In this way, I hope that English readers will be able more easily to judge the credibility of my argument in the light of subsequent development. I have attached a short postscript at the end of the book, stating briefly on a chapter-by-chapter basis the subsequent important development in the real world, as food for further thought, as well as referring to relevant new works of mine and others. In addition, I include my presidential address to the 1995 annual meeting of the Japanese Economic Association, drafted about the same time as the writing of this book, as an appendix. The address sketches an analytical framework for comparative institutional analysis that I relied on at that time. This framework has been refined since then and its outcome will be published soon in another book of mine. However, I thought that it would be a good companion piece to the present book, indicating its analytical and conceptual framework more explicitly than Chapter 1.

The translation of the book was financially supported by the Daido Foundation in Japan, for which I am grateful. I would like to express my greatest appreciation to Ms Stacey Jehlik for her careful and impeccable translation. She is masterful in both Japanese and English. She communicated to me any ambiguous or potentially misunderstandable expressions needing clarification and offered excellent suggestions. We worked well together, and I consider myself exceptionally lucky to have found her as my translator. Professor Kozo Yamamura of the University of Washington is responsible for introducing us. For that, as well as for persuading me to reconsider the possibility of an English publication of the book, I owe him my thanks. Finally, I am thankful to Andrew Schuller of Oxford University Press for persistently encouraging me to submit an English publication, for thinking of the title for the present English translation, for overseeing the speedy editorial process, and for our lasting friendship.

January 18, 2000
Stanford, California

Foreword to the Original Japanese Edition, 1995

The graduate economic program at Stanford University offers a field of study referred to as CIA. This field is not intended to teach the skills of intelligence activities for American global strategy, but rather aims at a new approach to economics called comparative institutional analysis, initiated by Paul Milgrom, Avner Greif, Yingyi Qian, John Litwack, and myself in 1990. I have already written about the background to CIA and our enthusiasm for it in a collection of essays entitled *Between Stanford and Kyoto* (Chikuma Shobo, 1991). Since then the CIA field has been growing steadily, and a few years ago we sent our first several Ph.D.s out into the world.

What CIA aims at, simply put, is as follows: because of the bounded rationality of economic agents, the asymmetric distribution of information among them, and the incompleteness of markets, etc., there cannot be any ideal economic system of universalistic value beyond time and across space. It would be fruitless to try to mechanically apply implications of the theoretical construct of the Walrasian general equilibrium model to such practical problems as how economic relationships between Japan and the USA are to be arranged, or how institutional reforms are to be made in the process of the transition from socialist economies to market economies, etc. Rather, we ought to admit the diversity in economic systems and analyze their sources and evolution, the comparative advantages and disadvantages of different systems, and the possible gains from diversity. In doing so it will not be sufficient to analyze market institutions alone but will be necessary also to analyze the interdependencies of institutions mutually interwoven in complex ways. Valuable tools for doing so are the analytical language that has accumulated through the recent development of economics of information, and the theory of games, contracts, etc., that is shared among economists all over the world. In a phrase, we may say that CIA aims at a "universalistic analysis of a diversity of economic systems."

Since the formation of the CIA field, I have wanted to write an advanced textbook entitled *Toward a Comparative Institutional Analysis*.

However, before launching this project, I became engaged in the organization of three international projects on comparative institutional analysis co-sponsored by the Economic Development Institute (now the Economic Institute) of the World Bank and the Center for Economic Policy Research at Stanford. These projects are on:

- *The Japanese Main Bank System: Its Relevance to Developing and Transforming Economies* (co-organized by Professor Hugh Patrick)[1]
- *Corporate Governance in Transitional Economies: Insider Control and the Role of Banks* (co-organized by Dr Hyung-Ki Kim)[2]
- *The Role of Government in East Asian Economic Development* (co-organized by Professor Masahiro Okuno-Fujiwara and Dr Hyung-Ki Kim)[3]

Through these research projects, I have had the opportunity of working with about fifty scholars from more than ten countries and of being practically trained in comparative institutional analysis.

Meanwhile, in the fall of 1994 I spent three months in Japan lecturing on the comparative institutional analysis of the Japanese economy together with Professor Masahiro Okuno-Fujiwara at the Faculty of Economics of the University of Tokyo. At the suggestion of Toyo Keizai Shinpo Sha, I decided to make use of this opportunity to summarize for students, as well as for general readers, what I had been thinking and teaching, learning from the above mentioned projects, publishing in academic journals, etc. The present book is the outcome. It has an interim report on the progress of CIA leading to *Toward a Comparative Institutional Analysis*.

While I was writing this book, the advocacy for deregulation was in full bloom in Japan. Although I am an amateur in political discourse, I attempt to state my own private view regarding institutional reforms in Japan in the final chapter from the viewpoint of positively assessing the diversity of the economic system. I dare to propose a somewhat different view from either the developmental stage view, which argues that "the Japanese institutional arrangements were effective at the developmental stage, but should be transformed into the more advanced type," the Anglo-American universalistic view, which argues that "the Japanese institutional arrangements are deviant and should conform to the global

---

[1] Published by Oxford University Press in 1994.
[2] Published by the World Bank in the EDI Development Studies series.
[3] Published by Oxford University Press in 1996.

standard in order for Japan not to be isolated in the global community," or the isolationist view, which argues that "the Japanese institutional arrangement is by itself a coherent one and foreign pressure for further opening is nothing but a nuisance."

In order to make the book accessible to as many readers as possible, I have avoided using mathematical formulations and detailed scholastic references. However, most of the theoretical assertions expressed are backed up by analytical work. For a more academic treatment on the subject and references, readers may wish to consult a book co-authored with Professor Okuno-Fujiwara based on lecture notes for the course on the comparative institutional analysis of the Japanese economy that we gave together, which will be published by the University of Tokyo Press.[4]

February 15, 1995
At Stanford

---

[4] *Keizai Sisutemu no Hikaku Seido Bunseki* (The Comparative Institutional Analysis of Economic Systems), Tokyo: University of Tokyo Press, 1996.

1

What Is Comparative Institutional Analysis?

ECONOMICS IN AN AGE OF DIVERSITY

Is there such a thing as a single, ideal, universal model for economic systems? Or, given that a single system absolutely capable of outperforming all others in all economic and social dimensions has never existed, could the very coexistence of and competition between diverse systems on a global scale be the source of significant economic gains? If it is theoretically possible to realize gains from diversity, then would every nation have the ability to create an economic system that contributes to and takes advantage of those gains? What kind of relationship would have to exist among economies for the gains from diversity to be realized?

As the economies of the world become more and more globally integrated, these are the kinds of issues we can expect to face in striving to understand and devise policies for the wide range of phenomena occurring in the economic arena. To approach these questions, this book adopts the perspective and methodology of the newly developed framework of comparative institutional analysis, rather than the framework of neoclassical economics often used in the past.

Comparative institutional analysis strives to discover the source of economic gains from diversity and the circumstances under which they are realized using the universal analytical tools commonly employed in the field of economics and shared by economists worldwide. In this sense, comparative institutional analysis leans toward an economics of pluralism.

NEOCLASSICAL ECONOMICS AS A UNIVERSAL MODEL?

Neoclassical economics idealizes the Walrasian model of perfect competition as the most efficient economic system. In this model, the diffusion of economically useful information among various firms and consumers does not hinder the attainment of optimal economic coordination. Rather, this school of thought suggests that, in complete markets where prices are perfectly adjusted by an invisible hand in response to differences in supply and demand, competitive behavior between economic agents will automatically result in an optimal economic allocation. Since the information needed for attaining optimal resource allocation can readily be summarized in the price vector and circulated throughout the entire system, such a system of perfect competition is believed to be more information-efficient than centrally planned economies that centralize more detailed information and calculate centrally an optimal production structure. (It is theoretically impossible to achieve optimal resource allocation by exchanging an amount of information that is smaller in dimension than the number of goods.)

The mathematical economics of the 1950s and 1960s struggled to find the conditions under which the Walrasian equilibrium, which would represent optimal resource allocation, could exist. Likewise, scholars of comparative economics such as Abram Bergson devoted themselves to the task of estimating the degree to which resource allocation under the centralized planning of socialism deviated from the standard represented by the Walrasian equilibrium.[1] Underlying these economists' passion was the belief that the ideal economic system could only be realized through the Walrasian competition, a framework compatible with individual freedom.

It was recognized, though, that the existence of monopolistic firms and the various failures of markets – evidence that a complete market had not been generated for all resources – distort resource allocation at market equilibrium. However, it was expected that such distortions could be corrected by the existence of a well-intentioned government that would enforce perfect competition and make up for the deficiencies of the market through tax and subsidy systems. Clearly, there is a contradiction between the belief in free competition and the expectation that an omnipotent government would exist to maintain that competition. This contradiction was resolved by asserting that the national government should guarantee only the establishment of clear ownership rights over all economic assets, including the environment. This would give economic agents incentives to engage in bargaining, thus resulting in the spontaneous generation of the market. Such libertarian views have gradually

---

[1] Abram Bergson, *The Economics of Soviet Planning*, New Haven, CT: Yale University Press, 1964.

gained acceptance, and have come to challenge views favoring direct government intervention in resource allocation. This theoretical trend, coupled with the disintegration of the socialist planned economies in the real world, seems to have paved the way for the model of perfect competition to become firmly established as the universal norm among economic systems.

CAN THE ANGLO-AMERICAN SYSTEM SERVE AS A UNIVERSAL MODEL?

The closest approximation to the Walrasian equilibrium model is the American economy – or, as it will be referred to in this book, the Anglo-American system. Government regulations are tolerant toward new market entrants, and oligopolistic collusion is monitored fairly closely. Only under this system is there so much mobility in the labor market, and is the market for corporate control rights, or takeover mechanisms, so highly developed. It is its resemblance to the model of perfect competition that is believed to lend the Anglo-American system a high degree of rationality and legitimacy.

For example, when Central Europe (e.g. Poland, the Czech Republic, Hungary) and the former Soviet Union embarked on the transition to a market economy, they chose the Anglo-American system as the model to emulate without considering the actual results it might produce. As will be discussed further in Chapter 6, the implementation of plans to privatize state-owned enterprises in Russia and Central Europe, where the Anglo-American system had been adopted as a model, did not even come close to producing a corporate governance structure characterized by outside stockholder control. Instead, it resulted in the widespread phenomenon of insider control, that is the acquisition of a large share of stocks by managers and workers. At the end of the communist era, the managers of state-owned enterprises had already carved out substantial controlling rights for themselves, while enterprises had provided economic and social welfare benefits to workers. It was these historical conditions extant at the outset of the transition that constrained the possible outcomes of the enterprise privatization process.

While historical initial conditions generally act as a constraint on the formation of economic institutions, however, they do not fully determine their later development. So why did the tendency toward insider control become embedded in firms against the will of the reform authorities in Central Europe and Russia? Most likely because the attempt to simply transplant the Anglo-American system, which had developed under its own unique historical circumstances, was, like mixing oil with water, ill-fated from the outset. As a result, the privatization process was heavily influenced by the legacy of communism. In other words, some merits of the Anglo-American system can be easily taken advantage of only if certain historical preconditions exist.

Public commentators and the mass media in Japan, who until a few years ago had bombastically declared that "Japan has nothing left to learn from America," are now great proponents of deregulation *à la* the Anglo-American system. They contend that the various institutions that have supported Japan's strong economy thus far, such as the lifetime employment system, the seniority wage system, and the main bank system, are now on the verge of collapse. These institutional structures may have been effective during the stages of economic catch-up, but now the Japanese economy is being aggressively pursued by other Asian economies, including China, and is losing its power to compete as a manufacturing nation. Meanwhile, Japan has also been outdone by the USA in the development of new technologies, as is exemplified by the information and communications industries. Thus waging a battle on two fronts, the Japanese system and its future vitality are dependent upon the introduction of reforms that allow freer competition, foster creativity in development, and facilitate the demonstration of entrepreneurial ability.

But what kind of system will follow deregulation and fill the void left by the demise of customary Japanese practices? According to analysts, the structure of the new system is far from obvious. It is likely that it will emulate some of the characteristics of the Anglo-American system. There is no doubt that the Japanese economy has reached a major plateau, but can it reform itself into a system capable of achieving a comparative advantage in the world market only by incorporating several positive elements of the Anglo-American model?

Though the Anglo-American system can be characterized as tolerant toward new market entrants, it is not completely devoid of regulations. Indeed, it has been formed out of its own distinct regulatory structure. This unique structure is composed of laws like the Glass–Steagal Act, which prohibits commercial banks from dealing in securities or holding stocks, and labor laws that prohibit employers from bargaining outside the framework of the union selected by the majority of workers. The regulatory structure generally reinforces the system when it is internally consistent with other systemic elements (a situation to be conceptualized later in this book as "institutional complementarity"). Thus, it is altogether unclear whether the regulatory structure supporting one system can approximate the regulatory structure supporting another system, or whether the two can be fused together into a consistent new structure.

This suggests that mere clamors for "deregulation" do not contribute much toward efforts by the Japanese economic system to reshape itself in a manner befitting the new international environment. We have to reconsider whether it is even possible, let alone desirable, for the Japanese system to move completely in the direction of the Anglo-American system.

AWARENESS OF INSTITUTIONAL DIVERSITY AND THE UNIVERSALITY OF ANALYTICAL TOOLS

I have suggested that the convergence of the various economic systems that exist worldwide, and a complete convergence toward the Walrasian model in particular, would be difficult because of the variance in historical conditions among economies and the need for structural consistency between regulations and other institutions. Given this, could there be a positive, pluralistic significance to the coexistence of diverse systems on a global scale? How can the potential economic gains from diversity be taken advantage of either on a global scale or within the framework of a single national economy? Comparative institutional analysis is a new field of economics that has evolved out of attempts to develop a basic economic approach to these kinds of questions. Though comparative institutional analysis rejects the universality of the Anglo-American model and suggests that diversity among economic systems be embraced, it does not propose that there is a unique logic for explaining each and every individual economy. Some in Japan would argue that the lack of international recognition for works by Japanese economists is a result of the uniqueness of the Japanese economy. If that were the case, the comparative advantages and historical lessons that may be offered by the Japanese economy would never become part of the international intellectual assets. An analysis of different economies should not be performed using terms and tools relevant only to a particular national economy, but should use terms and tools developed in the study of economics and shared by economists worldwide. (I am referring here to analytical terminology, not natural language.)

Fortunately, tools for analyzing economic systems from a perspective other than that of Walrasian theory, such as game theory, contract theory, transaction cost economics, and information theory, have developed rapidly over the past twenty years. This book has been written on the basis of these developments. It has been repeatedly ascertained, in the process of developing comparative institutional analysis, that these theories are not only effective for the comparative analysis of different market economies, but are universally effective in historical analysis and developmental economics, as well as in the analysis of issues facing transition economies, that is, economies in the process of transition from communism to market economics.

In analyzing diverse economies using a standardized method, comparisons of several economies can substitute for the "experimentation" factor usually lacking in the social sciences. For example, premature generalizations of theoretical hypotheses based only on observations of the Anglo-American or Japanese economic system may be disproved when applied to other economies. Comparing several economies is like increasing the sample size in an experiment, and comparative institutional analysis, like the testing process used in scientific experiments, aims toward the general understanding of economic systems.

But how is the theoretical premiss of comparative institutional analysis distinct from that of Walrasian theory which has looked to the model of perfect competition as the single universal system? The remainder of this book will attempt to provide a satisfactory reply to this question, but let us begin with an introductory response.

BOUNDED RATIONALITY AND ORGANIZATIONAL DIVERSITY

What does it mean to say that neoclassical economics is premissed on the perfect rationality of economic agents? Even in neoclassical economics, every economic agent (household, firm) possesses only a certain limited amount and type of information (e.g. preferences, a share of resources, and technological information as represented in the production/cost function). In that sense it is implicitly understood that each agent's information processing capabilities are limited. It then assumes that every economic agent makes rational choices (demand and supply) to maximize their objectives (maximization of utility and profit) while exchanging the information they possess through the medium of prices.

Comparative institutional analysis explicitly acknowledges the fact of "bounded rationality" or "limited rationality," conceptualized by Herbert Simon who stated that economic agents "intend to act rationally, but their ability to do so is bounded."[2] First consider the limitations on the individual's information processing capabilities. Individuals must acquire information about their environment to engage in consumption and production. Limitations on the individual's information processing capabilities, however, render the collection of a vast array of unrelated information unproductive, and make it necessary for individuals to invest in a particular set of skills that limits the range of information they manage and the methods they use for collecting and processing it.

A firm organization is comprised of such individuals. The information collected by individuals relevant to the firm's activities is exchanged internally and used collectively. This kind of organizational structure may be called the coordination scheme. There cannot be a single best coordination scheme that will be optimal in all situations, because perfect collective rationality will not necessarily be achieved no matter how many individuals with bounded rationality are amassed. In a changing environment, differences in the kind of information processing skills selected by individuals and in the organizational coordination schemes adopted will result in differences not only in the information available for use by the entire firm in pursuing its goals, but also in the productivity and competitiveness of firms. The cost function postulated as technological data in neoclassical models is endogenous to this approach (is treated as a variable that must be explained).

Chapter 2 shows that placing certain types of limitations on the information processing capabilities of individuals working in a firm yields five prototypical organizational modes found in firm coordination schemes: classical, functional, horizontal, and decentralized hierarchies, and the homogeneous team structure. Traditionally economists have viewed firm organization either as a "black box," as in neoclassical economics, or as a hierarchy (classical or functional), as portrayed by transaction cost economists such as Ronald Coase and Oliver Williamson.[3] In reality, however, firm organization embraces a complex intermingling of these basic prototypes. The important question of which of these prototypes is the most (information) efficient depends on factors including the type and degree of uncertainty in the organizational environment, the technological and

[2] Herbert A. Simon, *Models of Bounded Rationality: Behavioral Economics and Business Organization*, Cambridge, MA: MIT Press, 1982.
[3] Ronald H. Coase, "The Nature of the Firm," *Economica*, Vol. 4 (1937), pp. 386–405; reprinted in *The Firm, the Market and the Law*, Chicago: University of Chicago Press, 1988. Oliver E. Williamson, *Markets and Hierarchies: Analysis and Antitrust Implications*, New York: Free Press, 1975.

stochastic relationship between the various activities needing to be co-ordinated within the organization, and the distribution of types and levels of information processing capabilities (skills) throughout society. Chapter 2 aims to define the conditions that determine comparative organizational efficiency. Its conclusions will be used to explain the evolutionary differences between the organizational modes employed in Japanese and American firms, as well as the behavioral consequences of those differences. The crucial difference lies in whether information about the systemic environment pertaining to the overall activity of the organization is assimilated or differentiated among all of the members of the organization. The implications can be used to explain the comparative advantage (or disadvantage) of Japanese and American firms in the high engineering and information industries, as well as in mature industries like the petrochemical industry.

THE EVOLUTIONARY GAME AND THE FORMATION OF MULTIPLE STABLE EQUILIBRIA

Chapter 3 discusses implications of the limits of the individual's maximizing behavior as an element of bounded rationality using the framework of evolutionary game theory. It will address the question of why different organizational conventions prevail in different economies. Though the several basic modes of coordination are complexly integrated in actual firm organization, certain basic modes tend to prevail in individual economies. For example, in Japan an assimilated (shared) information structure or, expressed in terms of the evolutionary progression, the horizontal hierarchy mode, is prevalent. In America, by contrast, developments in information and communication technology have been accompanied by a shift from the long-prevalent functional hierarchy toward a new organizational form, referred to below as the decentralized hierarchy. Because these organizational modes have different degrees of competitiveness in different industries, the prevalent mode in the economy is one of the factors that determines the competitiveness of that economy. These organizational factors largely explain some of the phenomena of intra-industry trade (such as Japanese dominance in memory chips versus US dominance in logic chips) which are not explained by the comparative advantage argument of classical trade theory.

Those factors do not, however, explain everything. Let us say that the A-mode of organization is competitive in one industry, while the Z-mode of organization is competitive in another. Why doesn't an optimal mixture of these modes emerge within each economy? Conversely, why is there a tendency for a single particular organizational mode to become conventionalized in a particular country's economy, regardless of industry? For example, differences in firm organization between the automobile and software industries in Japan are no larger than those between their respective competitors in the USA. However, though the Japanese organizational mode is competitive in the automobile industry, it is a step or two behind the US mode in the software industry, especially in object-oriented software design. The US automobile industry has studied and adopted some Japanese organizational practices, but has done so by partially revising its traditional functional hierarchy. Likewise, there seem to be some major barriers preventing the implementation of the American organizational mode in the Japanese software industry. Why is this?

Evolutionary game theory suggests that, in addition to the constraints on individuals' information processing capabilities, there are constraints on their maximization calculation (implementation) capabilities. Before participating in a firm organization (before starting up a firm or accepting employment), each economic agent must make choices regarding the direction they will take in developing their information processing capabilities. Simply put, each must invest in a limited set of skills when pursuing formal education or technical training. For example, let us assume that the individual has to choose whether to invest in the skills needed for carrying out a specific function (functional skills) in any type of organization, or in general problem-solving and organizational communication skills (malleable skills) in hopes of honing skills useful in a particular context (contextual skills) after gaining employment in a particular firm.

In this case, given the limited rationality of economic agents, the kinds of skills a person will perceive to be most advantageous to invest in will depend on the prevalent organizational mode in the economy. For example, even a person who excels in some specialized skill may, if employed in a firm with a strong assimilated (shared) information structure, be treated according to the adage "the nail that sticks up gets hammered down," while a person who expects to attain a wide range of contextual skills will be overlooked in an organization with a functional hierarchy. Also, skill investment takes time. Even if it is known that a certain type of skill is the most efficient type for a particular organizational mode, that skill type will not become available in the market overnight.

Let us assume that every economic agent looks at the prevailing organizational mode in the economy, as well as the distribution of types and levels of information processing capabilities throughout the population, and then chooses to invest in the seemingly most advantageous skills. The choice to invest in either functional or malleable skills is what game theorists call a "strategy." Let us assume, however, that the choice of the optimal strategy is affected by a certain inertia or friction caused by the economic agent's habits or limited calculation and projection capabilities. This concept can be formulated and analyzed within the Darwinian evolutionary model of the survival of the fittest, which suggests that investments in the types of skill that will achieve the highest gain in the economy will gradually become prevalent. When there are two or more industries with different information-systemic characteristics, we know that there can be multiple evolutionary equilibria that are stable against minor mutations in skill choices made by economic agents. This emphasis on multiple equilibria is one of the major differences distinguishing comparative institutional analysis from neoclassical economics, which is concerned more with the uniqueness of equilibrium.

The equilibria that draw the most attention are: the Pareto equilibrium (the P-equilibrium), where the optimal organizational mode for each particular industry is applied within that industry and skill types that correspond to each of these modes are employed; the A-equilibrium, where the choice of functional skills becomes the prevalent strategy regardless of industry; and the J-equilibrium, where the formation of malleable/contextual skills becomes the prevalent strategy regardless of industry. The economic gains derived from the diversity of organizations can be maximized at the P-equilibrium. If there are two or more industries facing different technological conditions, only the consumption preferences of the population will determine the rank-order of the suboptimal A-equilibrium or J-equilibrium. Which of these equilibria will be achieved, however, depends largely on the historical conditions of the economy, though this does not mean that history controls everything. This is discussed further in Chapter 3, but it is worth pointing out here that, although the P-equilibrium is the most desirable equilibrium at which the economic gains from diversity are maximized, it is also the most difficult to be reached spontaneously in a nascent market economy.

INSTITUTIONALIZATION AND INSTITUTIONAL COMPLEMENTARITY

Let us imagine a situation in which the choice of a particular type of skill is becoming the prevailing strategy in society, though it is not yet in equilibrium in a strict sense. Economic agents with bounded rationality will then perceive the choice of that strategy to be generally advantageous for themselves. This perception comes from their awareness of the high probability that it is they who will end up bearing the costs of any loss incurred if the strategy they select turns out to be poorly suited to the particular firm they join and causes a decrease in that organization's coordination efficiency. Selecting a strategy that corresponds to the prevailing social strategy is referred to as "strategic complementarity" in game theory.

However, even in such a situation, "mutants," who are committed to strategies other than the prevailing strategy, and "reformists," who want to try moving beyond short-term gains, will emerge in various forms. The slight probability of the appearance of these invaders has interesting implications for game theory, which will be discussed later, but in the real world we tend to develop mechanisms for enforcing as rules those strategies that offer mutual complementarity in order to achieve strategy matching at low calculation and transaction costs.

These rules may take the form of tacitly obeyed traditions or social norms, or of well defined, legally enforceable rules. That is, the creation of institutions is seen as a way to make formal rules out of complementary evolving strategies. The existence of multiple equilibria may be accompanied by the formation of multiple institutional structures. Because the environment as well as the distribution of information processing capabilities throughout the population will naturally change, a particular institutional structure will yield imperfections over time even in the economy in which it was formed. Also, there is no absolute guarantee that the structure achieved will be the optimal one.

We cannot know what an institutional structure that embodies the P-equilibrium would look like in reality. However, we at least know that each element of the institutional structure is mutually reinforcing, or possesses the characteristic we are referring to here as institutional complementarity, corresponding to the strategic complementarity by which the structure was created. In this regard, an institutional structure will be resistant to environmental changes once it is formed. This accounts for the fact that the institutional structures of the world are not easily converging, even though the world economy is becoming increasingly integrated in terms of trade.

Chapter 4 attempts to explain this institutional complementarity using the example of Japanese corporate governance and the interdependence of the financial and employment systems that support it. Corporate governance is the structure of rights and responsibilities among the parties with a stake in the firm. Under the Anglo-American system, employees are outsiders who can be employed and discharged through the labor market, and the relationship between employers and employees is regulated by an employment contract. If the remuneration paid to employees is determined by the external labor market, then the maximization of the expected residual value after all contractual payments have been made is the same as the maximization of the value created by the firm. Because the legal residual claimants are stockholders, the problem with corporate governance under the Anglo-American system is that of controlling the managers so that the stockholders can maximize the stock price.

As readers have surely surmised, the assimilated (shared) information structure (or, in terms of the evolutionary progression, the horizontal hierarchy) and the J-equilibrium put forth earlier were patterned on the stylized facts of the Japanese system. Because the skills needed in organizations in such an economy are "contextual skills" that are useful in the context of a particular organization, the value of that economy, unlike that of an economy emphasizing functional skills determined by the market, cannot be assessed in the external market. That is, it can only be determined through internal bargaining. Further, in firms with an assimilated (shared) information structure, teamwork is the typical mode of operation and no individual's contributions to the organization can be clearly identified.

In this case, should the output of the team be distributed on the basis of shares determined in advance among the employees? Economics warns that this method of distribution creates strong incentives for some individuals to free-ride on the efforts of others. This happens because a "team," in economic terms, is an organization in which it is difficult to measure individual effort. This book suggests that the relative lack of free-riding in Japanese firms is attributable not to the absence of this moral hazard problem, but to the relatively effective operation of the institutional mechanism for controlling it.

These institutional mechanisms were what made up Japanese corporate governance, which I call "contingent governance," and they had institutional complementarity with financial institutions, especially banks, and the long-term employment system. Contingent governance refers to a governance structure agreed upon in advance by the parties concerned, whereby the control rights of the firm are entrusted to managers (insiders) promoted or selected through the internal personnel hierarchy as long as that firm is financially sound. If and only if the firm's financial position deteriorates, however, control rights shift automatically from the insiders to a "designated" outsider, the main bank.

Even under the Anglo-American corporate governance scheme, the CEO may be replaced if the financial position of the firm deteriorates. However, if blame for the business problems can be attributed wholly to the personal responsibility of the CEO, another insider may be appointed as CEO by the board of directors, or an "undesignated" outsider may submit a takeover bid. Even if a firm is financially viable, it is not unusual for an outside member of the board of directors to wield extensive power in the management of the firm (e.g. in the selection of a new CEO).

The uniqueness of contingent governance, by contrast, is that shifts in control rights between insiders and outsiders is contingent only on the financial viability of the firm, and that even decisions regarding who will seize control rights in the event of the financial deterioration of the firm are explicitly laid out ahead of time by the parties concerned. Once it seizes the control rights of the firm, the main bank must choose to either rescue the firm or liquidate it. This choice will likely depend on the seriousness of the firm's financial hardship and projections for its future recovery. In Chapter 4 I use the recently developed contract theory and supermodularity analysis to show that this kind of two-tier contingency structure is the second-best mechanism for controlling incentive problems in team-oriented organization schemes. The incentive effects of the contingent governance structure will increase if the re-employment value of employees who lose their jobs because of the dissolution or liquidation of the firm is low, or in other words if other firms also tend toward long-term employment such that workers have limited outside employment options. In that sense, the main bank system and the long-term employment system are complementary institutional structures that mutually reinforce the productivity of organizations that utilize an assimilated (shared) information structure.

Changes to the main bank system that have naturally occurred as a result of the internationalization of financial markets and the implications of these changes on corporate governance will be discussed in the following chapters. First, though, I want to emphasize the importance of a clear and full understanding of the theoretical basis of institutional complementarity to the discussions that follow.

THE INSTITUTIONAL COMPLEMENTARITY OF REGULATIONS

The role of the main bank in the contingent governance structure may, in one regard, be interpreted as the monitoring (collecting and evaluating information) of the firm's financial position on behalf of the other investors. An important question in the economics of information is, "Who is responsible for monitoring the monitor?" In this case, what incentive does the main bank have to carry out the role assigned to it under the contingent governance structure?

The main bank's active intervention in corporate governance is limited to occasions when the firm's financial position has weakened, and even on these occasions the main bank must bear the costs of restructuring or liquidating the firm. Depending on the circumstances, it may be less hassle for the main bank to seize collateral to collect its debt and withdraw from governance than to fulfill this role. However, the reason that it was rare for main banks to eschew their responsibilities in the heyday of the main bank system (from the early part of the high growth period to the mid 1970s) was because they were able to secure certain advantages – main bank rent – by carrying out the responsibilities of a main bank.

During Japan's high growth period, the source of this rent lay in the regulations of the banking authorities which strictly controlled entry to the position of city bank and exercised controls to keep deposit rates lower than the Walrasian equilibrium level while maintaining the real rate at positive levels. Kevin Murdoch, Thomas Hellmann, and Joseph Stiglitz differentiated this situation of "financial restraint" from the situation of "financial repression" characterized by high inflation and negative real interest rates.[4] In a situation of financial repression, wealth tends to shift from households (the saving agents) to the government, but in a situation of financial restraint, rents emerge in the banking sector. This difference has serious ramifications for developing economies. In the case of the former, nonproductive or rent-seeking behavior that focuses on acquiring rents distributed at the discretion of the government is stimulated among those classes or families with government connections. This phenomenon was often seen in Africa and Latin America in the 1970s.

In a situation of financial restraint, however, rents belong to intermediate financial institutions as profits, thus strengthening the business base and giving rise to fierce competition among intermediate institutions for the acquisition of deposits. Also, because loan interest is determined by

[4] Thomas Hellmann, Kevin Murdock, and Joseph Stiglitz, "Financial Restraint: Toward a New Paradigm," in M. Aoki, H. Kim, and M. Okuno-Fujiwara (eds.), *The Role of Government in East Asian Economic Development*, Oxford and New York: Oxford University Press, 1997, pp. 163–207.

the risk and bargaining power of the borrowing firm, through mechanisms such as requiring the firm to hold compensating balances, a portion of the rent is actually distributed to the borrowing firm. Consequently, rent-seeking behavior in a situation of financial restraint produces a growth bias manifested by deposit acquisition or debt expansion. The tendency toward financial restraint is widely evident not only in Japan, but also in Korea and other Asian economies, and there is growing interest in its implications for today's developing economies.

It goes without saying that this kind of rent potential served as an incentive for banks to attain the rank of main bank and carry out the responsibilities required by that ranking, but would contingent corporate governance be impossible without the creation of such rents by the government? Recent conclusions reached in the economics of information indicate that this is not necessarily the case. However, if there are no government regulations for entry, a different equilibrium, perhaps an equilibrium at which banks do not participate actively in corporate governance, may be possible. This suggests that institutional complementarity may incorporate government regulations. Thus, the internationalization of financial markets may result in a gradual loss of consistency among government financial regulations, and will test the effectiveness of the main bank system in corporate governance. This challenge will force reforms toward greater consistency and coherence in the overall Japanese system.

IMPLICATIONS FOR TRANSITION ECONOMIES

The role of the main bank in contingent corporate governance is to exercise ex post control when a firm's financial state turned out to be deteriorated. By contrast, the project evaluation conducted before financing an investment project can be called ex ante monitoring, while the continuous audits of the state of a business conducted after financing has been granted is called interim monitoring. Naturally, main banks play a crucial role in both of these. The main bank does not generally loan funds independently, but provides an average share of about 20 percent of a firm's total loans. However, the main bank has actually come to fulfill the responsibilities of the lead bank of a joint financing group because other financial institutions accept the judgment of the main bank on its project evaluation. In the golden age of the main bank system, the main bank played a considerable role in running the payment settlement accounts of the borrowing firm, thus giving the bank easy access to the information necessary for conducting interim monitoring. In contingent corporate governance, the main bank commits in advance to intervening if the financial position of the borrowing firm declines. The potentially costly risks to the main bank entailed in ex post intervention serve as an incentive for the main bank to perform its ex ante and interim monitoring functions in such a way as to prevent the financial decline of the borrowing firm.

Entrusting ex ante, interim, and ex post monitoring to a single intermediary, the main bank, is a distinguishing feature of the main bank system that sets it apart from other financial institutions. Under the Anglo-American system, ex ante, interim, and ex post monitoring are performed by separate, specialized intermediary or other institutions. For example, ex ante monitoring is performed by investment banks, commercial banks, or venture capital firms; interim monitoring is performed by analysts, market arbitrageurs, or investment fund managers; and ex post monitoring is handled by takeover bidders, or the bankruptcy court and reorganization specialists.

Integrated monitoring under the main bank system is believed to be exceptionally effective in the technological catch-up stages, such as during Japan's high growth period. This is because, in the evaluation of new investment projects, it is more important to determine whether or not the borrowing enterprise possesses adequate business and organizational skills for absorbing and refining imported technologies than to conduct a technical assessment of emergent technologies. Since the main banks had accumulated information on enterprises through their long-term relationship (interim monitoring) with them, they would be best qualified to perform the task of ex ante monitoring.

For a functionally diversified system like the Anglo-American one to work well, human and other resources for performing each of the specific monitoring functions have to be available in sufficient quantities. In postwar Japan such resources were unavailable, owing to the national-level control of financial affairs during the war. Consequently, it was more effective to channel scarce monitoring resources into the banks, and then entrust those banks with comprehensive monitoring functions. This kind of historical evaluation may offer some useful suggestions for corporate governance or financial system reform in economies currently trying to shift from central planning to market orientation.

As mentioned earlier, attempts in the transition economies of Central Europe and Russia to introduce outside stockholder control through the process of business privatization, and to transplant the Anglo-American corporate governance scheme, seem largely to have failed. Even though a grand attempt was made to wholly introduce functional monitoring through the market, it was not compatible with institutions inherited from communism such as the expanded rights of managers, the welfare function of firms, and the scarcity of outside monitoring resources. Chapter 6 addresses the problem of how to control the negative aspects of the "insider control" phenomenon resulting from the collusion of managers and workers in transition economies. This problem cannot be solved by the mechanical application of the main bank system, but instead requires a solution that is consistent with the evolutionary characteristics of transition economies. However, contingent governance theory, in which control rights automatically shift to an outsider if the firm loses its financial viability, provides a useful frame of reference from which to consider the problem of insider control.

There is another advantage to making banks bear the burden of monitoring firms in transition economies: that is, bank monitoring is compatible with various forms of firm ownership. The Anglo-American monitoring and governance structures presuppose that a firm's ownership rights are in principle tradable, and that a firm's value can be assessed by the market. However, in economies like China, where a gradual approach is being taken toward the transition to a market economy, various forms of ownership will emerge during the transition period. There are fully state-owned enterprises, partially state-owned enterprises, enterprises owned by local governments, listed enterprises, joint ventures, entrepreneurial enterprises, and worker-managed enterprises. It is not immediately clear who is supposed to exercise the ownership rights of corporatized state-owned enterprises, if an information-efficient securities market has not yet been fully developed.

However, any enterprise under any form of ownership must rely on bank financing if it lacks sufficient internal funds. Consequently, even if several forms of ownership coexist, it is still possible to construct a mechanism by which the deterioration of a firm's financial state automatically triggers the intervention of the bank as creditor. If a viable form of corporate governance is selected as the evolutionary outcome of this process, the transition will be able to proceed gradually, but it would be difficult to say that the existing banking system has either the capabilities or incentives needed for fulfilling that kind of role. Consequently, corporate governance problems in transition economies can only be solved in conjunction with banking reform. Since the issue of transition economies is one of the last significant economic structural problems remaining in the twentieth century, a new field of Transition Economics has emerged, drawing many economic theorists into its ranks. The methods used in comparative institutional analysis have the potential to contribute much to this field. As has already been pointed out, comparisons of several economies supported by analytical methods constrain the premature assertion of an unrefined theoretical proposition derived from a single economic perspective. Conversely, the ability to recognize regularities amidst the workings of seemingly disparate economic systems under different historical circumstances makes it possible to discern trends that might not otherwise be discovered in an exclusive analysis of a single economy. It is by virtue of these merits that comparative institutional analysis can make up for the lack of experimental proof that constrains the social sciences.

HOW CAN THE ECONOMIC GAINS FROM DIVERSITY BE REALIZED?

Earlier I suggested that there is a latent potential for realizing maximum economic gains by implementing different organizational modes corresponding to the specific nature of each industry. However, because of evolutionary pressures toward the survival of the fittest, there is a tendency for organizational modes to converge within a national economy, and for organizational diversity to manifest itself as differences in organizational conventions between nations. Diversity may gradually begin to appear within a single national economy due to the international reciprocation of learning, experimentation, and organizations, but it is uncertain whether the resulting structure will approach optimal diversity for that economy. In every economy the prevailing economic strategies are institutionalized in various forms, and these greatly impact a person's strategy for selecting a skill set in the competition for the survival of the fittest among individuals.

The final chapter, Chapter 7, discusses the various mechanisms by which the economic gains from organizational diversity may be approximated. First I analyze the gains from free trade. If we assume that there is an organizational mode that is best suited to each industry, an economy that develops a particular mode as its prevailing organizational convention can be expected to attain absolute industrial dominance in international trade in the industry to which that mode is best suited. However, the degree to which the world economy can realize gains from the existence of such economies will depend entirely on the relative size of those economies.

First suppose that a small nation, say the J-economy, develops an effective new organizational mode in a particular industry. The J-economy, which has carved out its own niche in developing this new organizational mode, may then be able to monopolize the gains from diversity as "quasi-rent." That is, as long as the quantity supplied by the J-economy is small, its international price will be maintained at a high enough level for production to continue even under the old organizational mode. Other nations will only begin to enjoy the gains of the J-economy's organizational innovation after the J-economy has grown to such a degree that its products have captured a certain share of the world market. However, unlike neoclassical economics, which treats the organizational mode of the firm as a black box, evolutionary game theory incorporates the element of organizational mode as a variable and thus suggests different implications regarding the gains from free trade. That is, the economic gains from organizational diversity will never be fully realized through free trade between economies that have conventionalized different organizational modes. For those gains to be fully realized, organizational diversity must be internalized within each economy.

What about the potential for diversification through foreign direct investment? If a J-economy that has developed an innovative organizational mode liberalizes foreign direct investment during the very early stages of its innovation, its newfound organizational innovation may be smothered by the infiltration of the world's prevailing organizational modes. However, if there are several economies of about equal size that have internalized different organizational conventions, each of which have a comparative advantage in the world economy, the internalization of organizational diversity may be achieved through economic integration (i.e. free movement of capital and labor) between them, or through the liberalization of foreign direct investment. Within these economies, international firms, being somewhat free from the restrictions of the capital and labor systems of the foreign nations in which they invest, may, through direct investments or joint ventures, serve as the carriers of forces that instigate the internal diversification of organizations. Economies with institutional structures that tolerate the entrance of experimental organizations, or that have the incentives and capabilities for developing information processing and communications technologies that simulate the workings of comparatively advantaged organizational modes, are likely to have the upper hand in being able to realize the gains from organizational diversity.

The USA, which once seemed to be a step behind Japan in the use of information on the factory floor in the manufacturing industry, seems to have largely overcome its comparative disadvantage in that arena by learning Japanese-style practices and developing remarkable information processing and communications technologies. As a result of the development of digital communications technologies and the standardization and outsourcing of parts, organizations are processing large quantities of data that extend beyond their immediate environments while trying to expand their coordination networks on a global scale. This is eroding the comparative advantage in the high engineering fields that Japan acquired by developing meticulous, precision-oriented coordination schemes within organizations and between groups.

China, on the other hand, has reached the brink of a period of rapid organizational reform by introducing its own corporate reforms, as well as large scale foreign direct investment projects and joint ventures. Once these reforms begin to take root, China will be in the advantageous position of a late developer, able to selectively adopt the organizational modes formed earlier in other countries. Japanese firms have moved significant portions of their established manufacturing bases into East Asian nations including China, and are in no position to back out now. Thus, their potential for acquiring the quasi-rent generated from the Japanese organizational mode is rapidly declining.

From the late 1970s to the late 1980s, the quasi-rents acquired by Japan were not retained solely in the hands of the major export firms. Redistribution systems like entrance barriers (which maintain domestic and overseas price discrimination) and the tax and subsidy systems made it possible for the burden of comparatively disadvantaged industries and interest groups to be borne by them. This mechanism can be called "bureaupluralism" in the sense that the vested interests of all parties are equally protected through the mediation of the bureaucracy. However, the reduction in quasi-rents arising from changes in the international environment is beginning to make it difficult for the structure itself to be maintained.

Under the system of bureaupluralism, internationally competitive enterprises drift away from bureaucratic protection, while comparatively disadvantaged industries in the domestic arena become increasingly dependent on bureaucratic protection. However, a solution to this dilemma is not likely to be reached by introducing the Anglo-American system in Japan, improving the business "manners" of the export industry, or building higher barriers against market entrance. In industries that have had the comparative advantage thus far, firms are being forced to critically assess their own business modes in light of the organizational and information innovations now occurring in the world in order to maintain their competitiveness in the high engineering industries. In comparatively disadvantaged industries, meanwhile, ensuring the coexistence of unconventional organizational modes by liberalizing entrance for both domestic and foreign firms will result in long-term economic gains. Of course, creating "internal diversity" within Japan may not be a very easy task under bureaupluralism, but postponing the public discussion of institutional reform measures that would lead in this direction can no longer be tolerated.

The concept of institutional complementarity developed in this book plays an important role in how we think about institutional reform. The interdependence of institutions does not necessarily mean that changes to the institutional structure should be carried out in "Big Bang" fashion, all at once. As mentioned in the earlier discussion of transition economies, efforts to take the Big Bang approach without any consideration of historical processes cannot but become mired down in historical constraints. Rather, finding the source of strategically important and politically feasible changes may open up opportunities to induce successive systemic changes by relying on "complementarity" between various institutions.

This raises additional questions. Is it possible to have institutional reforms, especially relaxed entrance regulations, that permit organizational reform and diversity, without forfeiting the comparative advantage that the Japanese organizational mode has had until now? The creation of a new organizational mode is needed, but under Darwinian pressure toward the survival of the fittest, how will it be possible to encourage the creation and institutionalization of dormant functional skills by a new generation? I believe that the institutional reform of corporate governance can be one important trigger for making this happen. This book will conclude by exploring the implications of lifting the ban on the holding company system to this issue.

2

Organizational Diversity and Comparative Informational Efficiency

IS THE PRODUCTION FUNCTION REALLY A TECHNOLOGICAL GIVEN?

In neoclassical economics, the firm is treated as a purely technological entity that hires land, labor, and capital and inputs raw materials and intermediate goods to produce goods and services that can be sold in the marketplace. The inner workings of the firm are treated as a kind of black box and are assumed to be determined by engineering factors that lie outside the scope of economics. The entrepreneur adjusts the amount of input into this black box and sells the goods produced from it at market prices so as to maximize profits. Thus, the input and output of the firm are determined entirely by the parameters of market prices. That is, the coordination of resource allocation is conducted almost solely in the marketplace through the medium of prices.

However, even the activities of firms that seem to be mere technological input–output relationships can generate different results depending on differences in how information is handled by the people involved. That is, differences in coordination within firms may very well be a major cause of productivity gaps between economies. If this were not the case, there would be no differences in competitiveness between firms or between economies within the same industry.

Take the petrochemical industry, for example. The naphtha produced from the crude oil refining process is further decomposed into intermediate components, such as off gas, ethylene, propylene, C_4 fractions, C_5 fractions, and heavy oil, which are then reconfigured into an array of derivative products in variable compositions. The possible compositions are determined entirely by technological relationships. These derivatives, through various manufacturing processes, are finally transformed into finished products including fertilizers, resin products, pharmaceuticals, fibers, paints, tires, film, semiconductor materials, solvents, and cleansing agents. Consequently, the selection of compositions produced from the various component materials greatly depends on how information pertaining to the demand for these various finished goods is applied.

This is not to say, however, that changes to the production plan in the upstream process are made according to a rationalized plan, implemented only after the firm collects market information relating to the demand for finished goods and calculates the optimal production composition. The information costs of collecting detailed information on the hundreds of thousands, even millions, of potential finished goods are prohibitively high. Assume that one firm were to effectively integrate everything from the upstream separation process to the derivative production and manufacturing processes, and that another firm were to specialize in the upstream separation process while establishing relationships with several independent downstream firms to which it would supply intermediate materials. Even if both firms operated in technologically identical industrial complexes, and even if both of their end-processing firms were facing the same market situation, a different coordination scheme would likely result in each. In the latter case, altering the supply plan would entail some form of negotiation with the downstream firms, thus yielding a time lag between the onset of changes in final demand and the alteration of the upstream firm's supply plan to accurately reflect those changes. Also, the behavior of each downstream firm would be affected by the fact that changes in the quantity supplied today would impact their negotiating power tomorrow, thus raising the question as to the degree of consistency between the supply plan and final demand.

The operational efficiency at a petroleum or nuclear power plant depends largely on how the firm copes with emergent events that arise in the normal course of operations. To what degree are the on-site operations teams granted discretionary power to react quickly? Is there a built-in structure by which information on an observed irregularity can be communicated laterally to other operating units, or would such a situation be handled only through a vertical command structure? The productivity of a firm may depend on the quantity and quality of information exchanged among a firm's administrative or production personnel, as well as on the structural allocation of decision-making authority and responsibility. Firms may be engineering entities, but they are also information systems.

Consider the automobile industry. In terms of the production flow, the auto industry is the exact opposite of the petrochemical industry. Instead of having many production sites for processed goods branching out from a refinery, many separately produced auto parts are channeled inward toward a final assembly line. Even so, though, thousands of different auto models can be produced from a single production line by varying the assembly of body types, colors, engine powers, transmissions, accessories, and other features. Under this arrangement, if the product composition is determined solely on the basis of early forecasts of market demand, forecasting errors will undoubtedly result in excess inventories of high-priced goods.

To decrease the costs of excess inventories, the product composition plan on the production line must be continuously fine-tuned to accord with actual consumer demand on the dealer floor. Some Japanese manufacturers construct information and communication systems between their dealer networks and their production sites so they can make any necessary adjustments on the production line up to seven days before assembly is scheduled to begin. Effectively fine-tuning the production composition also requires that a system be established for supplying thousands of parts to the assembly sites at the proper times. Such a system is called a *kanban* or "zero-inventory" system, and requires that the production-line installation sites order necessary parts directly from suppliers several times a day. This system caused paradigmatic shifts in the production organization of assembly industries in the 1970s and 1980s because it employed an information and communication system fundamentally different from the former Anglo-American system, under which a central parts procurement department ordered parts on the basis of the existing inventory.

As a final example, let us examine the impact of America's information technology revolution on the internal coordination schemes of firms. If the employees of an organization are linked together through a decentralized network that replaces the old mainframe-based system, and if digital communications between these networks expand, it will become possible for employees to have a hitherto unknown degree of access to data outside their own task units. Consequently, if the standardization and compatibility of parts continues as it has in the production of personal computers and object-oriented software, and if the production process is modularized, the need for comprehensive coordination schemes within organizations will likely decrease. This will be made possible by the digitalization of communication and air transportation, which will allow firms to quickly outsource the best standardized parts from anywhere in the world. Network based business coordination (other than the distribution of financial and human resources within the firm) will give rise to the phenomenon of virtual corporations that operate only in cyberspace and exist beyond the legal boundaries of corporations. The introduction of this kind of new coordination paradigm in the information industry seems to be having an impact on some manufacturing sectors as well. The auto industry, for example, is beginning to see a trend toward the common standardization of parts and toward the use of digital communication networks for used car parts transactions.

If firms could always select the most efficient coordination structure, or information system, based on the specific nature of the good to be produced, the results of that selection would likely be reflected by the production function (cost function). However, as will be shown in the next chapter, institutional factors do not always allow firms to select the most effective information systems. In Japan, the increasingly meticulous coordination schemes within firms and among fixed groups of firms has become so prevalent that flexible digital information sharing among firms is lagging behind. Part of the explanation for the sense of inadequacy haunting Japanese firms regarding their role in the formative stages of cross-industrial sectors like the internet industry may in part be a result of their having mismatched information systems.

It becomes necessary to explicitly treat the organization of a firm as an information system, and not merely as a "black box" embodying efficient technological knowledge. An understanding of today's economy, where complex technologies for meeting diversified consumer preferences have been developed, requires more than an analysis of how the market will affect the coordination of resource allocation. It also requires an analysis of the coordination that occurs within and between organizations through non-price media. A conceptual framework for conducting such an analysis is presented in the next section.

DIVERSITY OF INTERNAL CORPORATE INFORMATION SYSTEMS

The late Harvey Leibenstein was one of the first economists to draw the attention of economists to the fact that internal factors of firm organization have at least as much of an effect on the efficiency of an economy as on the coordination of resource allocation in the market (like the degree of oligopoly). He called the productivity differences that resulted from factors within the firm the *X-inefficiency*.[1] Leibenstein hypothesized that this inefficiency resulted from differences in worker response to incentives and coordination schemes within the organization, but he did not go so far as to explicitly study its origins. This explains his use of the rather enigmatic term "X-inefficiency."

This section focuses on intra-organization coordination and relies on the results of recent model analyses to raise questions about how it might cause differences in productivity between firms. In taking this approach, I do not mean to suggest that the incentive aspects of the organization are not important – on the contrary, the coordination and incentive elements are inextricably intertwined. The methodology for analyzing the two together, however, is not yet very well developed. Also, the incentive elements are already relatively well recognized, having been the target of much attention among economic theorists for the past twenty years. Much light has already been shed on this area, and some excellent work on the topic has already been produced. The relative theoretical importance of intrafirm coordination, by contrast, is not very well recognized because the Anglo-American scholars who have dealt with the issue have merely conceptualized the internal coordination scheme in terms of hierarchies. In reality, however, organizations may employ a coordination scheme that is not hierarchical in the strictest sense, and that is, in fact, more efficient than a strict hierarchical scheme under some conditions. This section first addresses the aspect of organizational coordination because it is linked to the development of my overall argument.[2] The incentive aspects are discussed in the following two chapters.

First, suppose that firms are organized as shown in Figure 1, and are made up of management and multiple individual operating units. In reality, the selection of the structure itself is the responsibility of the entrepreneur (or the management on behalf of the entrepreneur) and is based on an assessment of the market and the available technology, but let us here posit this structure as a given. The operating units will tentatively be called "task units" below. Figure 1 may also be viewed as a subsystem of the firm, not as an organizational chart of the entire firm.

---

[1] Harvey Leibenstein, "Allocative Efficiency vs. 'X-Efficiency'," *American Economic Review*, Vol. 56 (1966), pp. 392–415.

[2] As far as I am aware, Masahiko Aoki, "Horizontal vs. Vertical Information Structure of the Firm," *American Economic Review*, Vol. 76 (1986), pp. 971–83, was the first article to construct a comparative model of internal information systems as a source of productivity differences between firms. Later Hideshi Ito, Jacque Cremer, Roy Radner and Timothy van Zandt, and Phillipe Bolton and Mathias Dewatripont developed comparative models of various types.

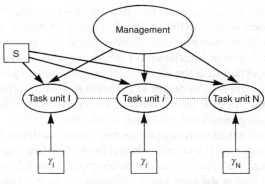

S: Systemic environment
γ_i: Idiosyncratic environment

Fig. 1 Basic organizational structure

Assume that task units perform their assigned mutually interrelated activities, and that management is responsible for supervising the coordination between these activities. The costs and returns of the firm's production activities will be affected by various uncertain factors that lie beyond the direct control of the task unit. These factors are called *environmental parameters* (external variables), and can be characterized as either "idiosyncratic" or "systemic" parameters:

Idiosyncratic environmental parameters

These are the environmental parameters that individually affect the costs and returns of the activities of each task unit. There are only as many as the number of task units.

Systemic environmental parameters

These are the environmental parameters that have a simultaneous external effect on the costs and returns of the activities of all task units.

Take the auto assembly line as an example. If the line stops, all the tasks connected to that line are affected simultaneously. Consequently, factors that have an effect on the continuous operation of the line are part of the systemic environment; factors that affect only a single task, such as the engine installation, are part of the idiosyncratic environment. As this example suggests, it is not always that easy to distinguish between the two in reality. One defective engine may be able to be dealt with individually on that site, but if a large quantity of poor engines is detected, the problem may affect the whole assembly line and may have an external effect on other task units as well. All that is actually needed for the following analysis, however, is the statistical correlation between each task unit environment. If the degree of correlation is high, the systemic environment will be more important than the idiosyncratic environment, while the opposite is true if there is a low degree of correlation. This conceptual distinction between systemic and idiosyncratic environments is useful in categorizing organizational coordination schemes.

Let us posit that environmental parameters vary randomly, but that the random distribution is known in advance by the firm (management). The realized value of the parameters can be observed in the information processing activities of the firm, but it will always include errors because of the bounded capability of the observers. To attain a maximum expected return, the firm selects the type and amount of good to produce and determines the activity level of each task unit by using the information it possesses "as a whole" most effectively. Consequently, the firm, in addition to engaging in production activities, also has to perform information processing activities. It has to collect information, which involves observing the environment and measuring parameters, and it has to make decisions regarding the nature and level of activity of each task unit in response. Information regarding the market for its products can be obtained through actual product sales. Task unit activities such as detecting, searching for the causes of, and resolving machinery breakdowns and monitoring control panels are simultaneously production and information processing activities. Accordingly, the production and information activities within a firm may be viewed as inseparable.

Organizational schemes differ depending on how these information processing activities are structured within the firm. First, assume that the entrepreneur or management has already determined the number and structure of task units based on prior knowledge of the market and technological environment. Given this, the problem becomes how to organize the ex post processing of information regarding the systemic and idiosyncratic environments so as to achieve the goal of maximizing returns. However, the bounded rationality of both the management and the task units that comprise the firm constrains the selection of organizational modes. Let us adopt the following bounded rationality assumptions.

1. Management knows the prior statistical distributions of systemic and idiosyncratic environmental parameters, but cannot observe the realized values of these parameters ex post with satisfactory accuracy and

timeliness. The basic responsibility of management is to select specific economic activities from a set of those characterized by the different stochastic distributions and to establish them as the organizational structure.

2. Each task unit can observe both the systemic environment and its own idiosyncratic environment, or can observe either one or the other, but their measurements of the realized parameter values will include observational errors. The size of those errors (variance) will depend on the information processing capabilities of each task unit. When task units observe both environments, their errors will increase per unit of observation time because their attention is split between observations.

3. Ex post information regarding the idiosyncratic or systemic environments that can be obtained at the task unit level cannot be transmitted accurately and immediately from the observing task unit to the management. Also, idiosyncratic information cannot be conveyed to other task units. This is "on-site knowledge" that can only be acquired and understood by personnel situated in that environment.

The importance of the "knowledge of the particular circumstances of time and place" available only to on-site personnel was emphasized by Friedrich A. von Hayek in his classical work, "The Use of Knowledge in Society."[3] However, Hayek did no more than suggest that on-site knowledge is put to the best social use through the decentralized price mechanism by which supply and demand derived from the individual use of that knowledge are translated into and disseminated as prices. The firm was still implicitly treated as a black box. If the management were omnipotent, capable of immediately collecting and understanding all on-site knowledge and of incorporating that information into its decisions on an up-to-the-minute basis, the internal coordination of the firm would certainly be taken as a given and posited outside the scope of economic analysis. However, in the large scale organizations that exist today, useful on-site knowledge is dispersed throughout the entire organization, and the assumption of an omnipotent management is not consistent with the premise of the importance of on-site knowledge.

What kind of coordination schemes are possible within an organization given (1) the limited information processing capabilities of task units, and (2) the impossibility of centralizing on-site knowledge? Five prototypes are presented below.

[3] Friedrich A. von Hayek, "The Use of Knowledge in Society," *American Economic Review*, Vol. 35 (1945), pp. 519–30.

First, the early stages of a market economy are dominated by a classical hierarchy wherein information processing authority is centralized in the entrepreneur/management. Adam Smith's pin factory is a typical example of this pattern. This was also contrasted against market coordination and was posited as the only organizational type by transaction cost economists such as Coase and Williamson.[4]

Classical hierarchy

Management chooses the activity levels of each task unit on the basis of prior knowledge of the idiosyncratic and systemic environments. Each task unit receives instructions from management regarding its level of activities and carries out these instructions with some error. This error occurs because of factors such as the presence of noise in the process of transmitting the instructions, limitations on the capabilities of each task unit to understand its instructions, and/or a lack of incentives to carry out the instructions.

However, in conjunction with the diversification of the market and technological advancements, on-site knowledge within the firm has also become more complex than in the classical pin factory. If the information processing capabilities of on-site personnel can be increased, the efficiency of the firm can be improved by adjusting hierarchical control such that on-site personnel are entrusted with processing and using ex post information regarding on-site environmental parameters.

Functional hierarchy

The task unit collects information regarding its idiosyncratic environment and makes its own decisions regarding its level of activity in accordance with organizational rules set out in advance. Organizational rules are established by the management on the basis of prior knowledge of the systemic and idiosyncratic environments.

The purpose of Frederick Taylor's principles of scientific management was to create clearly formulated rules regarding the various production processes and to train on-site workers to apply them. Also, recent neoclassical contract theory has undertaken the task of determining how to formulate remuneration contracts that serve to motivate workers to perform decentralized decision making.

As mentioned in the last section, the increasing use of digital communication will make it possible to transmit large quantities of data and to

---

[4] See n. 3 in Ch. 1.

convey information regarding the on-site environment or data needed for estimating systemic environmental parameters to each task unit. This will clear the way for the emergence of a more decentralized organizational mode such as follows.

Decentralized hierarchy

Management establishes rules for selecting the activities of each task unit based on prior knowledge of the systemic and idiosyncratic environments. Each task unit individually assesses the systemic and idiosyncratic environmental parameters, and makes its own decisions regarding its activities in accordance with the prescribed rules.

Though each unit may extract data regarding the systemic environment from a common information network, its utilization in decision making is modularized and differentiated among task units. An implication of access to systemic information by task units is the decentralized delegation of information processing that facilitates faster decision making.

This evolutionary pattern – from classical hierarchy to functional hierarchy, and from functional hierarchy to the decentralized hierarchy – has been heuristically assumed, but other evolutionary patterns may also be possible. For example, let us start again from the classical hierarchy, but assume that each task unit is performing approximately the same kind of task. That is, we assume that within the task unit the environmental parameters shared by all employees are of significantly greater importance than the idiosyncratic environmental parameters of each task unit. Take the primitive example of teamwork in which a team of workers loads cases onto a truck. In this case, a coordination scheme may develop in which systemic environmental information is jointly processed by the team, and activities are jointly selected on the basis of assimilated information. This may lead us to hypothesize the following prototype.

Homogeneous team

Task units collectively observe the systemic environmental parameter value, and specifically select and implement the activity level of each task unit on the basis of the shared knowledge attained. Private information regarding idiosyncratic environments likely to be possessed by each task unit will not be used in joint decision making.

However, if, in conjunction with the diversification of the market and technological advancements, the independence of individual task units increases, it may become necessary to process and use ex post information regarding the idiosyncratic on-site environments. This may result in the creation of the following rather complex organizational mode.

Horizontal hierarchy

While task units collectively observe the systemic environmental parameter value, they collect information on their own idiosyncratic environments separately. The selection of the level of activity at each task unit is made independently, on the basis of information attained and in accordance with the rules established in advance by management.

The term "horizontal hierarchy" is used to denote the nature of the information system (not the structure of authority), in the sense that collective processing of the systemic environment and separate processing of the idiosyncratic environments are layered, and the term is used to differentiate this mode from a hierarchy in the authority sense. The horizontal hierarchy and decentralized hierarchy seem similar in that under both modes task units simultaneously process information on both the systemic and idiosyncratic environments, but they differ in that, under the former, information regarding the systemic environment is processed jointly, while under the latter it is processed separately. As we will soon see, this organizational difference may cause decisive differences in organizational efficiency depending on technological factors.

COMPARATIVE INFORMATIONAL EFFICIENCY OF ORGANIZATIONAL MODES

The five organizational modes above were heuristically developed, but actual firm organizations consist of a complex mixture of differing degrees of those basic prototypes. However, understanding the circumstances under which each prototype has the comparative advantage is more effective than initially analyzing complex organizational modes and conducting theoretical and historical analyses on the process by which those modes were developed. When the coordination scheme of a firm selected on the basis of a particular organizational mode is expected to offer higher returns per unit of time than a coordination scheme based on a different organizational mode, given the same technological and environmental parameters, the former organizational mode is said to have a higher "informational efficiency" than the latter for that environment.

A comparison of the informational efficiency of the different prototypes depends not only the structure of each mode, but on the capabilities of the personnel involved in processing information within each mode. Consequently, to conduct a meaningful comparison of the informational efficiency of each organizational mode, first let us assume the same level of information processing capabilities of all personnel regardless of organizational mode. (The information processing capabilities of each economic agent can be indexed by the ratio of the prior variance of observation parameters to the variance of observation errors. Consequently, if the economic agent can observe the true parameter value with no errors, the capability index will be infinity, while if no information can be collected such that the variance of the observation error value is infinity, the capability index will be zero.) However, if information is collected on both the systemic and idiosyncratic environments as it is in a decentralized hierarchy or horizontal hierarchy, the observation error of each environmental parameter per unit of time will increase because of the increased diffusion of attention and training costs.

The following definition is important in comparing organizational modes. If the marginal returns from the activities of each task unit increase when the activities of other task units also increase – that is, if the marginal productivity of one task unit can be improved by the increased activities of other task units – we say that "technological complementarity" exists between those task units. (Later in this book I will introduce the important concepts of "strategic complementarity" and "institutional complementarity." The concept of "complementarity" plays a major role in this book. Its basic definition is essentially the same as the classical definition provided by Edgeworth.) In software development, for example, if the system design can be improved by feedback from the encoding task unit, the latter can be said to be complementary to the former. There is also strong complementarity between the task units on the assembly line of an auto assembly plant – if more engines than frames are produced, the extra engines are useless.

Conversely, imagine a situation in which the marginal productivity of the activities of each task unit declines as a result of increased activities at other task units. Given the limitations on tangible and intangible organizational resources within a firm organization, the task units compete exclusively for their use. In this situation, we say that task units have "resource competitiveness" (or substitutability). For example, these kinds of competitive relationships are likely to exist between the various downstream manufacturing processes that use the intermediate materials of a single oil refinery as their raw materials. As stated in the last section, the increased potential for outsourcing that has arisen from the development of digital communications technologies and the standardization of parts weakens the complementarity of task units within a firm and intensifies the competition between task units for personnel with specialized skills. If neither technological complementarity nor resource competitiveness exists between task units, they are said to be technologically separable.

When the degree of uncertainty in the idiosyncratic environment is especially high compared with that of the systemic environment (that is, when the ratio of the variance of the idiosyncratic environmental parameters to that of the systemic environmental parameters is high), the stochastic correlation between task unit environments will be low. In the reverse situation it will be high. The most information-efficient organizational modes, assuming equal information processing capabilities, are shown in Figure 2 against the two dimensions of the technological relationship (complementarity/resource competition) and stochastic correlation between task units.[5]

For example, if the stochastic correlation between task units is low, the informational efficiency of the functional hierarchy is not only greater than that of the classical hierarchy, but is greater than all of the other organizational modes. This will be most efficient regardless of the technological relationship between task units.

Conversely, when the stochastic correlation between task units is especially high, the optimal organizational mode depends on the technological relationship between task units. If the task units are complementary, the most information-efficient organizational mode is the homogeneous team in which the systemic environmental parameters are observed jointly and decisions are made on the basis of shared information. In this case, ignoring private information relating to the comparatively stable idiosyncratic environments is not at all detrimental. It seems paradoxical that the exclusion of private idiosyncratic information helps the decision-making outcome, but the balance of coordination between complementary activities is better maintained if the task units choose their actions on the basis of shared information. If task units compete for resources, the most information-efficient organizational mode will be one in which task

---

[5] For precise modeling and proof leading to the results summarized in Figure 2, see Masahiko Aoki, "An Evolving Diversity of Organizational Mode and its Implications for Transitional Economies," *Journal of Japanese and International Economies*, Vol. 9 (1995), pp. 330–53. See also Jacque Cremer, "Common Knowledge and the Co-ordination of Economic Activities," in Masahiko Aoki, Bo Gustafsson, and Oliver E. Williamson (eds.), *The Firm as a Nexus of Treaties*, London: Sage, 1990, pp. 53–76.

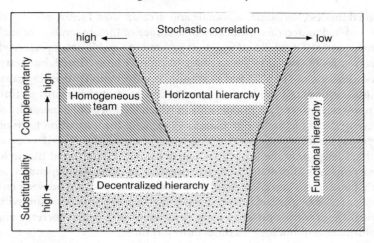

Fig. 2 Distribution of optimal organizational modes
From Chapter 3 onward, the "homogeneous team" and the "horizontal hierarchy" will be referred to together as *assimilated information structures*, while the "decentralized hierarchy" and "functional hierarchy" will be referred to together as *differentiated information structures*.

units independently observe the systemic environment and use that information to make decentralized activity decisions based on differentiated information. In this case, if shared information were to be used to adjust task unit activities, the limited resources of the firm would be too quickly exhausted by competing activities of task units.

When the systemic and idiosyncratic environments have an approximately equal effect on the costs and returns of the task units, that is, when the stochastic correlation between the task units is neither high nor low, a more complex organizational mode will have to be introduced. When technological complementarity exists between task units, information needed for decentralized decision making can be most efficiently supplemented by first having task units jointly observe the systemic environment, and then having them independently observe their own idiosyncratic environments. When there is competition for resources between task units, the most efficient solution is for each task unit to independently observe both the systemic and idiosyncratic environments, and to use the information obtained to make decentralized decisions.

Because of the limited information processing capabilities of task units, the diffusion of the task units' attention under these two organizational modes (horizontal hierarchy and decentralized hierarchy) may be considered to decrease the degree of accuracy of the observation of each environment. Given the information processing capabilities of personnel, economies of specialization in observation may be sacrificed, but better coordination can be achieved as a result. As information processing capabilities evolve and the level of information generated per unit of time improves, however, the middle area in which the horizontal hierarchy or decentralized hierarchy dominates will expand. If information technology and the information processing capabilities of individuals develop to a high level, only the horizontal hierarchy and decentralized hierarchy will remain as information-efficient organizational modes, depending on whether there is complementarity or resource competition between task units. These two organizational modes are the most capable of surviving when the information processing capabilities of workers increase and information technology becomes more advanced.

Thus far we have taken the organizational structure of the firm as a given. In reality, however, it is a variable selected by the management. The selection of the basic organizational structure of the firm is largely related to the processing by the management of prior information regarding the systemic environment. Assume that management divides the feasible range of activities into several groups according to the strength of the statistical correlation of environmental variables that have an effect on each of the activities. That is, groups are divided such that we can assume that the activities in each group are strongly influenced by their common systemic environmental parameters. Management then assesses the profitability of each activity group on the basis of market information regarding supply and demand for each product, and makes decisions as to which of these to internalize and which not to internalize depending on the financial and organizational resources available. Specifically, they make decisions regarding the diversification of products as well as decisions regarding the establishment of divisions in the company and the acquisitions and sales of corporate assets. Activities involving these kinds of decisions will be called "managerial leadership."

Managerial leadership is a function of the owner or management of the firm regardless of the organizational mode of the firm. Under a functional hierarchy or a decentralized hierarchy, the managerial leadership and the information processing of the task units are clearly differentiated and specialized. Also, because the responsibilities of the task units are clearly delineated by function, it is relatively easy to merge or divide them. Consequently, firms that employ either of these two organizational modes can flexibly reorganize by reassessing the systemic environmental parameters between potential activity groups and restructuring the organization.

By contrast, in a homogeneous team (and to some degree in a horizontal hierarchy) task units jointly participate in information processing activities, and conduct ad hoc decision making based on ex post information. Consequently, it is not altogether clear what the responsibilities and jurisdiction of each task unit are. One of the functions of management in this kind of organization is to provide an organizational framework for conducting joint information processing and decision making. Alternatively, one may say that management mediates such joint activities. As a result, the division of authority between the management and task units is not clearly defined, and this fact may affect the style of managerial leadership. That is, because information processing is closely interconnected among task units once their activities have been internalized within such an organization, the firm will lack the relative flexibility needed for reassessing the systemic environmental parameters and restructuring the organization accordingly.

ORGANIZATIONAL EVOLUTION AND TRANSITIONS IN THE INTERNATIONAL COMPARATIVE ADVANTAGE OF INDUSTRIES

How well do the theoretical predictions posited in the previous section explain the actual comparative advantage between economies? Let us once again examine the examples raised earlier in this chapter focusing on the concepts of "complementarity" and "stochastic correlation." Historically, the classical hierarchy has become prevalent in the early stages of the formation of firm organizations in every economy. This occurs because these early stages tend to be characterized by the skewed distribution of information processing capabilities among the population. In many cases economic agents with the incentives and information processing capabilities to become entrepreneurs form firm organizations and fulfill the role of management themselves. In these stages, the processing of prior information regarding the systemic environment, such as the market for products or inputs or the issues of factory design, is thought to be of the utmost importance to the firm's profitability, while the processing of ex post information regarding the nano-environment of the task unit does not yet play a significant role in the management of the firm.

However, as information processing capabilities at the lower levels of the hierarchy begin to improve, technologies can be introduced that require more complex judgments for the accomplishment of each task. The demand for increased levels of military production and productivity during the Second World War served as a major impetus for the introduction of "scientific management" practices in the USA. The essence of this movement was to systematically train workers to be able to respond to relatively complex problem-solving situations that might arise in the workplace. All workers were trained to follow the instructions in a manual for handling situations that might arise in their individual tasks. The stochastic correlation between tasks was systematically and technologically controlled, and the systemic environment within the factory was stabilized through the calculated division of tasks, the introduction of highly reliable mechanical structures, and the use of inventory stockpiles as shock absorbers. This fine-tuning of the functional hierarchy allowed the USA to achieve unparalleled productivity improvements in the traditional manufacturing industries such as automobiles, steel, and chemicals, making America the world leader in manufacturing until the late 1970s.

Meanwhile, a different pattern of development emerged during the Second World War in Japan. Japanese industry before the war was also characterized by a classical hierarchy, and technology was imported primarily from Europe. However, the demarcation of tasks at the task unit level, with the exception of the advanced shipyards and armories, was still ambiguously defined. The shortage of labor caused by the large number of enlisted personnel made it even more difficult to deal with mechanical breakdowns, parts shortages, absenteeism, and other emergencies through task specialization. Status distinctions between workers and foremen, or white and blue collar employees, rapidly blurred during this period. The tendency toward information sharing in workshops was intensified by the workers' factory control movement which spread immediately after the war. When managers regained control in the 1950s, they could not but honor the worker autonomy that had spontaneously evolved in the workshops.

A situation in which the stochastic correlation between tasks is high may be found only in primitive teamwork situations. In the modern firm, the idiosyncratic information requirements that each worker faces individually may be equally important as those they face as a group. Indeed, the goal of Japanese managers from the 1950s to the 1960s was to fuse the group approach that had spontaneously evolved on the shop floor with the scientific management techniques that had been developed in the USA. The resulting approach was a horizontal hierarchy.

As already mentioned with regard to the auto industry, when many parts have to be assembled into various products on a single assembly line because of the diversification of products, strong "complementarity" exists between tasks. Suppose that the interruption of the assembly line has a simultaneous external effect on the productivity of each task unit using the line (hence the importance of the systemic environment). It would be best if the information regarding the systemic environment – for example the problems arising in a particular task unit, such as mechanical breakdowns or defective products that could lead to assembly line interruption – were shared between related on-site task units and immediately used to jointly devise solutions to the problem. However, operating complex machines also requires that individual workers master their particular tasks.

A major reason for the international competitiveness of the Japanese automobile industry from the late 1970s to the mid 1980s was that, unlike the USA, which had implemented a functional hierarchical organization all the way down to the workshop level, the Japanese introduced elements of a horizontal hierarchy onto the assembly lines. This allowed the workshops to innovatively handle the increase in complementarity between operational tasks that had been brought about by the diversification and increased complexity of products. The information structure between the assembly plants and the subcontracted parts suppliers under the *kanban* system included elements of a horizontal hierarchy, in that information regarding the timing of the parts supply was shared by both parties while the processing of information regarding the parts production was left to the individual subcontractors. In other words, the automobile industry is organized as a multilayered horizontal hierarchy.

Japanese firms have also developed the horizontal hierarchical organizational mode in product development. Because there is a high degree of uncertainty regarding the outcome of development activities, the flow of operations from upstream to downstream processes does not necessarily have to run a straight course downward like a river. It is beneficial to use a constant feedback loop in which information obtained in the later stages of operation (such as the testing, manufacturing, or marketing stages) is relayed back to the earlier stages in which design modifications can be made. This is an instance of complementarity. To make use of this complementarity, Japanese firms did not align upstream and downstream task teams in a strictly hierarchical order from development to manufacturing to marketing, but developed a horizontal hierarchy in which those processes overlap. Also, engineers have largely similar backgrounds in terms of their university education, and the mutual ties between engineers are semi-permanent due to the lifetime employment system. Further, in addition to the common practice of having some engineers transfer to management positions at the manufacturing site midway through their careers, there is a tendency toward a high degree of information sharing within the development team and between the development team and the manufacturing site. Japanese firms were able to take advantage of these organizational features to greatly upgrade their technological standards in the 1980s in manufacturing industries such as automobiles, machine tools and electrical machinery, referred to hereafter as the high engineering industries.

In technologically mature industries such as the petrochemical industry, by contrast, Japanese firms are not competitive. In these industries, the uncertainties between processes can largely be handled through technological means. Consequently, efficiency in these industries requires that a structure exist in which the idiosyncratic information regarding the downstream market for processed goods is quickly and accurately assessed, and then reflected in the upstream supply system of intermediate materials. In industries like these, where the stochastic correlation between the downstream processes is low, an organizational mode that integrates the downstream processes with a traditional functional hierarchy will continue to be effective. Internationally competitive American and European petrochemical firms possess such a structure.

Alfred Chandler, the famous management historian of the Harvard Business School, collected and scrutinized data on the surging acquisitions and sales of corporate assets in America in the 1970s and 1980s.[6] He found that the industries in which corporate restructuring really contributed to improved productivity and profitability were the chemical and pharmaceutical industries. Chandler found that the secret to success in these industries was that the information-processing and decision-making functions involving the acquisitions and sales of corporate assets were performed not by the investment bankers of Wall Street, but under the leadership of the managers themselves who possessed industry-specific information about the industrial market and the technological environment. Thus, it was discovered that strong entrepreneurial leadership was complementary to a functional hierarchical structure.

By contrast, the trend in Japanese firms, which tended toward organ-

---

[6] Alfred Chandler, Jr, "Competitive Performance of US Industrial Enterprises since the Second World War," *Business History Review*, Vol. 68 (1992), pp. 1–72.

izational modes characterized by a high degree of information sharing, was for small and medium-sized petrochemical enterprises, which specialized in their own derivative products or unique processed goods, to flourish. Production coordination based on the immediate use and processing of information regarding the market environment was hampered by repeat transactions between multiple firms technologically integrated within a single industrial complex and by an excessive reliance on on-site coordination for safety. Also, the coexistence of firms that tend toward exclusive homogeneous team structures makes it very difficult to restructure the industry through mergers or through the acquisition or sale of assets.

Organizational reforms by Japanese firms in the high engineering fields posed a serious challenge to American industries, which had merely internalized the functional hierarchy across the board in all but venture businesses. The US information industry seems to have met this challenge by achieving a breakthrough in organizational mode in the 1980s and 1990s. Recall that the operations of the functional hierarchy are based on specialized skills for handling idiosyncratic information and decentralized decision making based on it. The comparative advantage of this organizational mode may be enhanced by expanding the scope of information processing to the level of the systemic environment and thus facilitating its evolution into a decentralized hierarchy. If the technological complementarity between tasks within a firm can be strategically decreased, this mode will be all the more effective. In the end, technological complementarity and stochastic correlation are not just technological givens, but variables that can be selected by a business.

For example, suppose that products are highly complex, but designed in such a way that they are assembled from standardized parts produced in module so that the diverse needs of customers can be met. Take, for example, the production of object-oriented software or downsized computer and communications systems. If supplies of standardized parts can be procured in a timely manner through outsourcing, the interdependence of intra-organizational units would be greatly reduced and scarce intra-organizational resources, such as design capabilities and financial resources, could be utilized more effectively. Needless to say, the realization of such a decentralized hierarchy has become a reality through the revolutionary developments of digital (i.e., Internet) communications and global transportation.

Another important outcome of this development is that each task unit sometimes has direct access to vast amounts of data lying outside the boundaries of the firm. In nascent industries such as the Internet, where standards for future methods of transmitting information have yet to be established, the interplay of many firms drawn from different sectors will result in the natural selection of de facto industry standards. The formation of industry standards cannot be completely internalized within a single firm. Thus, continual access to data regarding the wide-ranging systemic environment is vital to the productivity of each task unit, in this case individual entrepreneurial firms. However, extending with the tradition of the functional hierarchy, the sharing of data regarding the systemic environment does not necessarily imply the uniformity of interpretation of data. Rather, the interpretation of data would differ depending on the specialized function of each entrepreneurial firm. This modular information structure prevents all of the task units from expending resources in the same direction.

In the Japanese economy, the sense of powerlessness that haunts Japanese firms regarding their role in the formative stages of the internet industry comes from the limitations of an organizational mode based on information sharing and coordination within individual firms or designated groups of firms. However, once industrial standardization takes root, there may come a time when Japanese firms will be able to take advantage of their engineering capabilities.

If intra-industry productivity differences between economies depend at least to some extent on the organizational mode of intrafirm information processing, why are the optimal organizational selections not made simultaneously by all economies? Why instead do innovations in organizational mode occur and develop within a particular economy? Why is it that, even though mutual learning of organizational modes occurs between economies, differences in organizational modes within a particular industry seem to be largely consistent across economies? For example, why did the *kanban* system innovation in intra- and interfirm information systems occur in Japan? Likewise, why did reforms in R&D organizations in the software and bio-tech industries, as well as leadership in the formation of internet standards, occur in the USA? Why has the Japanese petrochemical industry not learned the industrial organizational modes used in the Europe and the USA? Can industries ever compensate for their delayed development? Comparative institutional analysis focuses on the analysis of institutional diversity and provides an analytical framework from which to approach these questions.

3

The Evolutionary Game and Multiple Equilibria

THE FORMATION OF FUNCTIONAL/CONTEXTUAL SKILLS AS A STRATEGY

At the end of the last chapter, I indicated that the classical hierarchy characterized by centralized information processing tends to be the prevalent organizational mode in the early stages of corporate formation. As the continued social accumulation of information processing capabilities proceeds, and the importance of systemic or task unit environmental parameters on the internal activities of the firm increase due to the development of increasingly complex and advanced technologies, firm organization will start to develop complex organizational architectures. However, comparative economic research reveals that economies have distinct characteristics that predispose them toward information sharing or the specialization of information processing. As a result of these predispositions, economies make qualitatively different modifications to the basic hierarchical structure.

For example, modifications to the classical hierarchy principle under the Anglo-American system have tended toward the gradual incorporation of diffused information processing. On the one hand, the information processing functions relevant to the strategic decision-making role that involves upper-level judgment are concentrated in the hands of management; while on the other, the information processing functions relevant to operations have been delegated to the functionally specialized lower-level units according to prescribed rules. If the technological complementarity between task units is strong, the diffusion of information processing will be limited to the idiosyncratic environment of the task unit (functional hierarchy), while if weak, the diffusion of information processing will extend to the systemic environment (an element of the decentralized hierarchy) with the support of developments in digital communications technologies. The distinguishing features of these modes are that, regardless of the level of hierarchy, the information processing functions of each employee are clearly specialized, and the information formed is differentiated. Consequently, when there is no particular need to distinguish between the two from this point forward, I will refer to these two modes together as "differentiated information structures." I will refer to the information processing capabilities useful under these organizational modes as "functional skills."

On the other hand, modifications to the classical hierarchy in Japan have tended toward first incorporating elements of the homogeneous team on a trial-and-error basis, and later establishing them permanently. Japanese firms have had to adapt to an incessantly changing environment, from the prewar emphasis on heavy and chemical industries, to the wartime shift to war-related production and extreme labor shortages, to postwar recovery and the high growth period. However, given the relatively undeveloped social accumulation of entrepreneurial leadership skills needed for strategic decision making, as well as of various kinds of functionally specialized skills, adaptation to such an environment could not have been accomplished through the evolution of the Anglo-American-style differentiated information structure. The various problems that continuously arise in the process of adapting to the environment were approached collectively either by the organization as a whole or by the task unit as a whole. The functional responsibilities of each individual were not clearly demarcated, and collective ad hoc problem solving techniques prevailed. Through this trial-and-error process of problem solving, effective techniques were identified and gradually established as organizational routine. Recent research conducted by Takahiro Fujimoto reveals that even the *kanban* system emerged gradually from among the ad hoc problem solving techniques employed in task units to deal with the unanticipated jumps in demand that occurred during the high growth period.[1] The homogeneous team will eventually develop into an even more advanced form, the horizontal hierarchy, which includes elements of the functional information processing of the employees' idiosyncratic environments. When there is no particular need to distinguish between the homogeneous team and the horizontal hierarchy below, I will refer to them together as "assimilated information structures."

Effective information processing capabilities in an assimilated information structure, especially in its advanced form, the horizontal hierarchy, include the ability to improve information sharing through

[1] Takahiro Fujimoto, *The Evolution of a Manufacturing System at Toyota*, Oxford and New York: Oxford University Press, 1999.

communication with one's colleagues within the organization, the ability to perform flexible task assignment in adaptation to environmental changes, and the ability to deal with what Kazuo Koike calls on-site "emergent events," such as mechanical failures or the detection of defective products, on an ad hoc basis.[2] These are the wide-ranging skills needed for monitoring both the systemic and the idiosyncratic task unit environments. Such skills are called "contextual" skills because they can be learned and accumulated specifically within the context of a particular organization. Preparatory training prior to entering this kind of workplace should emphasize general problem-solving and communication skills. We will call these preparatory skills "malleable" skills, as they are the raw materials that can be formed into specific contextual skills in any organization.

I stated above that functional skills are effective under differentiated information structures while contextual skills are effective under assimilated information structures, but the converse is also true. That is, the type of skills in which an economic agent chooses to invest will depend on the prevailing organizational mode. If the differentiated information structure is prevalent, economic agents will expect to receive a higher payoff from investing in some kind of functional skill. If they were to invest in malleable skills in this case, prevailing organizations would not immediately recognize the economic value of those skills and would not try to employ those contextual skills within their organizations. If the assimilated information structure is prevalent, however, economic agents will expect to receive a higher payoff from investing in malleable skills. Economic agents who invest in specialized functional skills and insist that they be put to effective use may be treated according to the adage "the nail that sticks out gets hammered down." That is, it is important that the organizational mode and skill types match (are compatible).

The problem is that, as discussed in the last chapter, a particular organizational mode will not be the most information-efficient mode in all industries. The best possible option would be to have a pluralistic economy in which different organizational modes are selected in accordance with the particular market and technological environments facing each industry. However, a look at today's economy reveals that an optimal

---

[2] Kazuo Koike, "Skill Formation Systems in the US and Japan," in Masahiko Aoki (ed.), *Economic Analysis of the Japanese Firm*, Amsterdam: North Holland, 1984, pp. 44–76; "Learning and Incentive Systems in Japanese Industry," in Masahiko Aoki and Ronald Dore (eds.), *The Japanese Firm: Sources of Strength*, Oxford and New York: Oxford University Press, 1992, pp. 41–65.

distribution of organizational modes has definitely not been achieved. Rather, there is a tendency for a single organizational mode to prevail and become established as a convention within each economy. Is this merely a short-term transitory phenomenon? Can long-term adjustments of supply and demand or the natural selection of optimal organizations make it possible to achieve gains from organizational pluralism over the long term? To consider these questions, we first need to formulate a theory for explaining why different organizational modes prevail in different economies. We will use evolutionary game theory as our analytical tool.

The first economist to apply evolutionary thinking to the idea that each economic agent does not need to possess perfect rationality in order for the economy to approach an optimal state was Almer Alchian. This approach, followed by the famous essay on methodology by Milton Freidman, suggested that, if each economic agent attempts to emulate the strategies of those who succeed through trial and error, the most rational choice is likely to be selected through the process of natural selection within the economy.[3] If that were the case, an optimal pluralistic economy could be expected to develop everywhere. The analysis in the next section, however, leads to a somewhat different conclusion.

FORMATION OF MULTIPLE SUBOPTIMAL EQUILIBRIA: THE J-EQUILIBRIUM AND THE A-EQUILIBRIUM

Suppose there are two types of industries, V and M.[4] The V-industry is characterized by technological complementarity in production and a high stochastic correlation between task units. Accordingly, the assimilated information structure is information efficient and holds absolute advantage. The differentiated information structure has a low informational efficiency in this industry. The M-industry, by contrast, is characterized by resource competition in production technology and a low stochastic correlation between task units. Consequently, the differentiated information structure is informationally more efficient than the

---

[3] Armen A. Alchian, "Uncertainty, Evolution, and Economic Theory," *Journal of Political Economy*, Vol. 58 (1950), pp. 211–21. Milton Friedman, *Essays in Positive Economics*, Chicago: University of Chicago Press, 1953.

[4] A more rigorous treatment of the materials described in the rest of this chapter is found in Masahiko Aoki, "Organizational Conventions and the Gains from Diversity: An Evolutionary Game Approach," *Corporate and Industrial Change*, Vol. 7 (1998), pp. 399–432.

assimilated information structure and holds absolute advantage. Suppose the products of the V-industry and the products of the M-industry are complementary in terms of consumption (e.g. the VCR industry and the multimedia/software industry). That is, if both products are not supplied simultaneously, their utility will decline.

Assume that time runs continuously and that at any moment in time a firm is formed by the matching (coupling) of two economic agents. One of these agents is the entrepreneur, who selects an organizational mode, and the other is the worker, who possesses a certain type of skill that can be utilized by the entrepreneur. For the sake of simplicity, let us distinguish the two merely on the basis of whether they invested in "functional" or "malleable" skills and assume that they are identical in other respects. If they are a match and both possess malleable skills, an assimilated information structure will be formed, while if they are a match and both possess functional skills, a differentiated information structure will be formed. In any industry, if these two agents are mismatched with one possessing malleable skills and the other possessing functional skills, the productivity of the corporate organization formed by their coupling can be assumed to be very low. These assumptions are shown in the simple cost matrix in Figure 3. For example, in the V-industry, if the agents are a match and both possess malleable skills, the cost will be 10 dollars per unit produced, but if they are mismatched, with one possessing malleable skills and the other possessing functional skills, the cost will be 50 dollars per unit.

Suppose the products of each industry are sold in a perfectly competitive market. Regardless of the type of firm in which they were produced, there will always be one price per product. Owing to consumption complementarity between the two types of product, the price of a product whose relative supply has decreased will rise relative to the other product. Assume that the net returns – the product price minus actual production

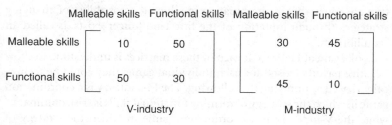

Fig. 3 Cost matrix

costs – are shared equally by the two economic agents that comprise the firm. These are the payoffs of the economic agents.

It is up to each individual to decide which type of skill to invest in and which industry to enter. Assume that the formation of a firm, or the matching of economic agents, is random at each point in time. That is, an economic agent who invests in a particular skill type and chooses to enter a particular industry can be expected to encounter all agents who chose the same industry with equal probability. This is an assumption of random matching. (Even if we relax this assumption and replace it with the assumption that each economic agent will be relatively more likely to encounter other economic agents with the same skill type, the basic theoretical argument below still stands.) Given this situation, each economic agent will "strategically" choose a skill type and industry to optimize their own payoffs, given the constraints of their bounded rationality.

Assume that the economic agent, at each point in time, knows which selection of industry and skill type will bring the highest "average" payoff in the population as a whole. Even among agents that choose that skill type and industry, discrepancies will arise in ex post payoffs as a result of random matching; but the agent is only looking at an average. Assume that economic agents try to emulate the strategy of "the fittest," but encounter some friction in doing so. For example, agents equipped with functional skills are mobile across industries because of the universal value of their skills across firms, but switching to contextual skills that yield a higher average payoff requires waiting for the next generation of workers to choose that skill type. Likewise, it will take time for agents who have converted their malleable skills into contextual skills in a particular industry to move into another industry. Because the dynamics of this friction-filled imitation of the fittest is analogous to the evolutionary process by which the fittest survives through natural selection, they may be referred to as Darwinian dynamics. Under Darwinian dynamics, the situation in which the expected payoffs of every member of the population are equal, that is, the situation in which the possibility of changing strategies through imitation of the fittest no longer exists, is called an "equilibrium."

Look again at Figure 3. If each of these matrices is understood to show negative payoffs (costs) for each individual game, they could be technically viewed as implying the following. The M-industry is a coordination game in which the strategy of forming functional skills is "risk dominant," while the V-industry is a coordination game in which the strategy of forming malleable skills is "risk dominant." The "risk dominant" strategy is the strategy that will produce the highest payoff when there is an equal probability for matching partners to choose either of the two strategies. Consequently, if these games are played independently, there is a high probability that the risk dominant strategy will be selected by the players.

Here the situation becomes slightly more complex, however. Because the products of the two industries have mutual consumption complementarity, their relative values will vary depending on the relative quantity supplied. If we introduce general market equilibrium theoretic elements and merge the two intra-industry coordination games into a single model, the coordination of the strategy becomes more complex. Because the actual payoff (price minus costs) of the players of the unified coordination game is affected by the market price for the product, even the selection of a strategy that is not risk dominant in one industry may produce a higher payoff. For example, let us assume that the majority of the population is composed of individuals that possess functional skills and that all of them move into the M-industry where those skills are risk dominant. If this happens, the quantity of products supplied from the M-industry will increase, and their price will fall. On the other hand, because the relative price of the V-industry, which has consumption complementarity with the M-industry, will rise, workers will now perceive it as profitable to enter the V-industry. There is no need to switch from functional to malleable skills in order to enter that industry. Doing so would increase the risk that there would be a mismatching with socially prevalent functionalist strategies. That is, if the majority of the population invests in functional skills, the expected payoffs from selecting the same strategy, regardless of the technological state of the industry, are high. In this case, functional skills are said to have "strategic complementarity." This is true even if the matching of contextual skills is technologically more advantageous to the V-industry. By contrast, if the majority of the population invests in contextual skills, they will become strategic complementary.

Though this scenario assumes only two industries and two types of skills, an analysis of an evolutionary game with this kind of strategic complementarity reveals that there are actually as many as nine equilibria. The several among these that are especially important are called "evolutionary equilibria." These are equilibria at which, even if a few "invaders" that deviate from the equilibrium strategy appear, and even if "random mutations" from the complementary strategies occur in the skill selection of economic agents, in the end Darwinian pressures will force these into alignment with the equilibrium strategy. There are three economically significant evolutionary equilibria. (There is also one pathological evolutionary equilibrium and five unstable points of equilibrium, but they are not economically significant.)

P-equilibrium

This refers to the Pareto-optimal situation in which firms employ the organizational mode most suited to their particular industry; that is, where firms in the V-industry internalize an assimilated information structure served by economic agents equipped with contextual skills, and the M-industry internalizes a differentiated information structure served by economic agents equipped with functional skills (that is, a situation in which it is impossible to raise the payoffs of some agents without sacrificing those of others).

A-equilibrium

This is the situation in which all firms in both the V-industry and the M-industry are organized as differentiated information structures comprised of economic agents equipped with functional skills.

J-equilibrium

This is the situation in which all firms in both the V-industry and the M-industry are organized as assimilated information structures comprised of economic agents equipped with contextual skills.

In this stage of analysis, where factors of agents' future expectations and experiments are ignored, historical initial conditions will determine which equilibria will be reached. This is called "path dependence." As already postulated, the A-equilibrium is likely to be reached in an economy in which a significant portion of the population is equipped with functional skills, while the J-equilibrium is likely to be reached in an economy in which a significant portion of the population is equipped with malleable skills. At either the J-equilibrium or the A-equilibrium, a single organizational mode will emerge. Unless pluralistic initial conditions prevail in which economic agents equipped with functional skills and agents equipped with malleable skills coexist in a significant ratio, the Pareto-optimal P-equilibrium will be difficult to achieve. Under Darwinian dynamics that involve strategic complementarity, it may be possible, depending on historical conditions, for there to be a development whereby economies converge toward a stable sub-Pareto-optimal

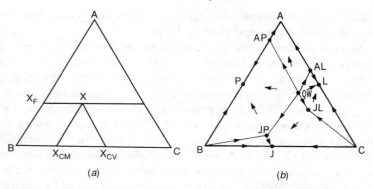

Fig. 4 Evolutionary game equilibria

Note: Figure 4(*a*) graphically represents the existence of multiple equilibria under Darwinian dynamics and the path dependence of their formation. This triangle is called a two-dimensional simplex, a device for showing the distribution of three-dimensional variables in two dimensions. Each side represents the size of the population, and distances from point B toward point A and from point C toward to point A represent the proportion of economic agents in the population equipped with functional skills. Because functional skills are formed as specialized skills independent of a particular organization, economic agents equipped with those skills can move instantaneously between industries. That is, because their payoff will be equal regardless of the industry they enter, there is no need to show explicitly their distribution between industries.

Because contextual skills, on the other hand, are formed within the context of a particular organization and do not allow for costless mobility between industries, their distribution between industries needs to be explicitly shown. A distance from point B toward point C represents the proportion of the population of agents equipped with contextual skills working in M-industry, while a distance from point C toward point B represents the proportion of the population of agents equipped with contextual skills working in V-industry. Let us tentatively assume that the population distribution of the economy is represented by point X (in part (*a*)). From this point, we draw a straight line parallel to each side of the triangle. When this is done, segment $\overline{BX}_F$ represents the proportion of economic agents with functional skills in the economy, segment $\overline{BX}_{CM}$ represents the proportion of the population equipped with contextual skills working in the M-industry, and segment $\overline{CX}_{CV}$ represents the proportion of the population equipped with contextual skills working in the V-industry.

Figure 4(*b*) uses this device to show the location of each equilibria. The A-equilibrium, where the entire population specializes in functional skills, is represented by point A. The J-equilibrium, where the entire population specializes in contextual skills, is represented by point J in the middle of the bottom side of the triangle. The portion of the bottom side of the triangle from that point to each of the points B and C represents the relative distribution of the population that works in both industries. The Pareto or P-equilibrium can be represented by a point located on line $\overline{BA}$. At this equilibrium point, segment $\overline{BP}$ represents the proportion of the population equipped with specialized skills working in the M-industry. The L-equilibrium is a pathological equilibrium in which the least efficient matching is sustained in both industries (i.e., the M-industry employs the relatively inefficient assimilated information structure and the V-industry employs the relatively inefficient differentiated information structure). The areas containing points A, J, P, and L, indicated by arrows pointing to the equilibria, are called the "basins of attraction" for their respective equilibria. That equilibrium. The Alchian–Friedman conjecture, which was not based on an explicit analysis, was incorrect on this point.

As readers have surely surmised from the use of the terms "J-equilibrium" and "A-equilibrium," Darwinian dynamics can be used as a theoretical device for explaining some aspects of the formation of different prevailing organizational modes in Japan and the US. From this perspective, the differences in prevailing organizational modes in these two countries may be regarded as a result of different "evolutionary equilibria" evolving out of unique historical circumstances. The workplace environment in Japan, a latecomer to capitalistic mass production, was initially saturated with elements of primitive teamwork (assimilated information structure). As mentioned earlier, collective ad hoc adaptations were widely attempted to deal with the continual environmental changes that the Japanese economy experienced from the war time period to the postwar period of high economic growth. Through this process, the formation of contextual skills became more and more prominent, and as a result the assimilated information structure of organization became established in the economy across industries.

In America, however, immigration acted as a mechanism for supplying new workers and served as a "self-selection process" of independently minded laborers. There was little incentive for these workers to develop contextual skills. Skill formation, through professional, technical, or vocational training, was specifically designed to increase the market value of the individual. As functional skills were accumulated throughout society thanks to the scientific management movement and the mass popularization of higher education resulting from the GI bill, a shift gradually occurred away from the classical hierarchy characterized by centralized information processing by management, to a differentiated information structure of organization. This shift was evolutionarily consistent with historical conditions.

It is important to point out, however, that, although the formation of

is, when historical initial conditions lie within one of these areas, Darwinian dynamics eventually results in a convergence toward the corresponding equilibria. Even if these equilibria have been temporarily disturbed by the invasion of a small group of mutants, they will be restored as long as the disturbance remains within one of these areas. That is, these four equilibria are evolutionary equilibria. The QW-equilibrium is a quasi-Walrasian equilibrium where all economic agents equipped with either functional or contextual skills can expect equal payoffs in both industries, but it is an unstable equilibrium that is referred to as the source in dynamic terms. The others – AP, JP, JL, and AL – are unstable equilibria that are called "saddle points."

organizational modes in Japan can be explained to a large degree by the phenomena of path dependence, this does not simply imply that the development of the Japanese organizational mode is "backward." As was made clear in the analysis of the comparative informational efficiency of organizations presented in the last chapter, neither the American nor the Japanese mode of organizational equilibrium is Pareto-dominant. The two organizational modes have different advantages in different industries. Some scholars feel that while the Japanese organizational mode was efficient in the stages when Japan was playing catch-up with the Western economies, it now needs to be brought into alignment with the Western system. However, as is evident from the Darwinian dynamics-based analysis, it is not altogether clear that it is possible to shift from the Japanese-style J-equilibrium to the American-style A-equilibrium. Besides, even if such a transition were possible, doubts remain as to whether it would be desirable. Japanese productivity in the high engineering industries might be lost with the disintegration of contextual skills.

An even more crucial implication to be derived from a Darwinian dynamics-based analysis is the potential existence of a pluralistic system (the P-equilibrium) that surpasses both the A- and the J-equilibrium. The problem, rather, is how the entire global system can move toward a more efficient Pareto-optimal situation characterized by organizational diversity. We will return to this problem again in Chapter 7. In preparation for that discussion, the remainder of this chapter will use the framework of the evolutionary game to review several basic theoretical problems regarding the possibility of equilibrium shifts.

HISTORY, FUTURE PROJECTIONS, AND STRATEGIC MUTATIONS

In the last section, we assumed that economic agents are shortsighted, viewing as optimal those strategies that assure them the best average payoff in the present. In that case, the selection from among multiple equilibria is entirely path dependent. But aren't economic agents free from the entanglements of history? Can't they play an antonomous role in choosing their own destinies?

Suppose that a portion of the population has the same future expectations. Suppose that their expectations for payoffs from each skill type do not merely project future payoffs that are equal to current average payoffs, but project changing future payoffs (capital gains). To the extent that the present value sum of expected payoffs for a particular skill type is relatively large, the number of agents selecting that strategy will increase. If we trace an evolutionary path toward an equilibrium at which those expectations are fulfilled, and if they start off far from any equilibrium point, somewhere between the J-equilibrium (or A-equilibrium) and the P-equilibrium, either equilibrium may be approached depending on initial expectations. In other words, the equilibrium path can bifurcate.

Accordingly, even if the majority of the population invests in contextual skills, if enough people possess an entrepreneurial spirit and still consider an investment in functional skills to be more efficient from the perspective of the future of the M-industry, there may be cases in which organizational diversity is ultimately realized. The likelihood of this happening will increase to the extent that a society has a thriving entrepreneurial spirit and that economic agents tend not to underestimate future payoffs and take a long-term view of business. In other words, the degree of freedom from historical constraints will rise. Conversely, if the costs of mismatching are high, there is a higher likelihood that historical constraints will restrict future choices.

Another mechanism that theoretically can reduce the deterministic nature of historical constraints is the continuous and random appearance of mutants – agents that deviate from the "boundedly rational" strategy of imitating the optimal strategy, or in other words the invasion of economic agents that ignore strategic complementarity in their behavior. As already defined, evolutionary equilibria are stable against strategic mutations, or the invasion of mutants. Several such equilibria were shown to exist under Darwinian dynamics. Even at an evolutionary equilibrium, however, the simultaneous occurrence of mass mutations by a critical mass of the population can cause an economy to shift to a different evolutionary equilibrium.

Refer once again to Figure 3. Assume that the preferences of the population are such that about half of the entire monetary gross income is spent on products from the M-industry, while the other half is spent on the V-industry. That is, the price elasticity of final demand for each product is 1. At the J-equilibrium, if 4.5 percent or more of the population were simultaneously to mutate from the conventional strategy by developing evolutionarily unfit functional skills, the economy would shift to the P-equilibrium. At the A-equilibrium, if 7.0 percent or more of the population were simultaneously to mutate from the conventional strategy by developing heretofore unfit malleable skills, the economy would transition to the P-equilibrium. At the P-equilibrium, by contrast, transitioning to the J-equilibrium would require that more than 20.5 percent of the population mutate from a strategy of developing functional skills to one of developing malleable skills, while transitioning to the A-equilibrium would require that more than 18.0 percent of the population shift from a strategy of developing malleable skills to one of developing functional skills. The minimum proportion of mutants in the total population needed to move from one evolutionary equilibrium to another is called the "cost of transition" from the former to the latter. Sample figures for these transitions are shown in Figure 5.

These sample figures indicate that the Pareto-optimal P-equilibrium is the most resistant to mass simultaneous mutations. In other words, the cost of transitioning from the P-equilibrium is the highest. This generally holds true and it has important theoretical implications, which will be discussed shortly. We also know that the costs of transitioning from either the A- or J-equilibrium, where the skill distribution throughout the population is completely asymmetrical, to the other, are exceptionally high.

It is important to reiterate that evolutionary equilibria are stable against the mutations of a few economic agents. Transitions from one evolutionary equilibrium to another may occur if a critical mass of considerable size simultaneously changes strategies. Consider next what

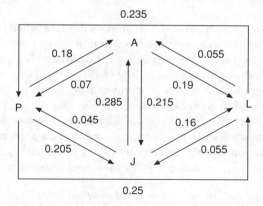

Fig. 5 Cost of transition

would happen if each member of the entire population were to mutate from the evolution-theoretic calculations and experiment with different strategies with a small probability. That is, assume that, instead of imitating the strategies of the fittest, economic agents chose from among the possible strategies randomly.

In such a situation it is possible, though with only a very small probability, that a group of economic agents of the size needed to cause a transition from one evolutionary equilibrium to another would simultaneously experiment with the corresponding strategy. As a result, the economy might move back and forth between multiple equilibria. Over the long term, however, the economy would probably spend the most time near a single evolutionary equilibrium. Our model suggests that, once the economy were to enter the vicinity of the Pareto-optimal P-equilibrium, the probability that it would remain there would be high since that is the equilibrium most resistant to change.

Recent research by Michihiro Kandori, George Mailath, and Raphael Rob offers such theoretical insight with respect to models in which agents from a finite population experiment with random strategies at a discrete time interval.[5] However, it is still not known whether a similar property can hold with a large population (which can be approximated as a continuum) of agents revising their strategies on a continuous time scale. There may be a high relative probability that the economy in this model would also make the transition to and rest at the Pareto-optimal P-equilibrium over the very long term, but if it were to start off at another evolutionary equilibrium, the transition would be likely to take an extraordinarily long time.

The findings of Kandori et al. can most readily be applied to problems of coordination between a relatively small number of people such as in the situation they use as an example in their study, the choice of computers among students in a dormitory. The realistic probability of disparate, random experiments in a large economy causing such a major change as an equilibrium shift is very low, and discretion must be used in drawing realistic implications for the dynamics of a particular economy from these theoretical results. Rather, in actual large economies, a phenomenon may emerge that restrains the operations of the mechanisms studied by Kandori et al. This phenomenon is "institutionalization."

[5] Michihiro Kandori, George Mailath, and Raphael Rob, "Learning, Mutation, and Long Run Equilibria in Games," *Econometrica*, Vol. 61 (1993), pp. 29–56. See also H. Peyton Young, "The Evolution of Conventions," *Econometrica*, Vol. 61 (1993), pp. 57–84.

INSTITUTIONS AS THE CODIFICATION OF EVOLUTIONARY EQUILIBRIUM STRATEGIES

If the dynamics of an economy that starts out with a fixed set of historical conditions reinforces the complementarity between specific strategies and approaches the corresponding equilibrium situation, establishing rules to enforce the adoption of those strategies will serve to reduce social and individual costs. First, if adopting an equilibrium strategy is turned into a rule, the information costs involved in adopting that strategy, such as the costs required for each economic agent to gather information and make evolutionarily fit calculations, will be reduced. Second, controlling the invasion of mutants will also reduce the resource costs resulting from equilibrium disturbances (mismatching). "Institutionalization" can be conceptualized as "the codification of evolution equilibrium strategies." Its implementation will be largely consistent with the incentives of individual economic agents in the vicinity of the equilibrium point. Thus, the social costs of rule enforcement may be lower than the information costs mentioned earlier. Under these circumstances, institutions will be sustainable and will contribute to the stability of the economic system.

Rules may be established as a legal system or may consist of customs or spontaneous moral codes. For example, contextual skills may be accumulated through continuous cooperative relationships between workers, but organizational conventions such as the seniority wage system or lifetime employment system also provide workers with incentives to form these skills. Case laws that make it difficult to terminate employment contracts give workers confidence in the corporate commitment to long-term employment. Under the Anglo-American system, on the other hand, MBA programs and other job training institutions aimed at training people with specialized skills have been institutionalized, while property rights to jobs based on seniority are recognized under collective agreement. In this kind of economy, investing in specialized functional skills will clearly produce the highest economic payoff. The real choice comes down to collecting information regarding the institutionalized market for each specialized skill, and determining what "type" of functional skill investment will yield the highest net returns.

If the institutional structure of a particular economy reflects equilibrium strategies in its underlying evolutionary game, complementarity is likely to exist between the elements of that structure. That is, the operations of one institution will be reinforced by the existence of other institutions. This is referred to as "institutional complementarity," a concept that will be examined in detail in the following two chapters. If institutional complementarity exists in an economy, attempts to change one institutional element independent of other elements will have only a limited effect. Because the institutional structure is like a big puzzle, attempts to arbitrarily replace pieces one by one will result in a loss of integrity of the whole picture. The institutional structure is by nature a conservative, inertia-driven entity. It contributes to the maintenance of a certain evolutionary equilibrium, but also makes it difficult to spontaneously make the transition to the optimal Pareto-equilibrium by suppressing the invasion of mutants and the mutation of skill choices within the population.

Though the institutional structure is inertia-driven, the structure and environment of the economic game underlying it will be affected by the development of production and information processing technologies as well as by the globalization of financial transactions. The distribution of skills throughout the population and incentives to form certain skills may be affected by the expansion of the educational system and other institutions of learning, the development of communication technologies, an increasing moral tolerance for experimental strategies, and international population mobility. The location of potential evolutionary equilibria is likely to be affected by these factors. A great many people probably hope for new organizational modes to be formed, but the skill-type matching that would make that possible may be hindered by organizational inertia or the underlying institutional structure. That is, institutional inertia may hinder the economy from moving toward an equilibrium of the organizational mode made possible by the distribution of (potential) skills throughout the population.

It may be useful, if somewhat superficial, to construct an analogy between skill types and genotypes, and organizational modes and phenotypes. Recent findings in the field of genetics suggest that a significant number of mutations are potentially stored in gene types without any remarkable changes in their phenotypes. Many of these changes are evolutionarily neutral or slightly inferior. However, if drastic environmental changes occur, the stored mutant genes may become more adaptable, making it possible for the sudden generation of new phenotypes.[6] In society, too, changes in the distribution of potential skills underlying the

---

[6] Motoo Kimura, *The Neutral Theory of Molecular Evolution*, Cambridge: Cambridge University Press, 1983.

prevailing organizational mode may also be accumulated for the reasons explained above. However, the fact that the accumulation of skill changes in society often remains untapped is due more to the fact that mechanisms of institutional conventions control the trigger of organizational change than to the fact that the accumulation of skill changes is neutral toward evolution as in biology.

Under these circumstances, people will at least vaguely sense the need for organizational change and diversity. However, achieving organizational diversity will be difficult without simultaneous changes in the complementary institutional elements that support the existing organizational convention. Consequently, effective institutional change requires that the expectations of a significant portion of the population regarding future change be coordinated. That is, the potential for institutional evolution depends largely on a society's cultivation of the entrepreneurial spirit. However, if the future expectations of economic agents are not coordinated well, their current behavior will be constrained by existing institutional complementarity, and conservative inertia will remain prevalent.

4

Corporate Governance and Institutional Complementarity

RETREAT OF THE MARKET FOR CORPORATE CONTROL

The concept of corporate governance, which was virtually unheard of in Japan until very recently, has become the focus of more and more attention. The term "corporate governance structure" originally referred, in the Anglo-American context, to the legal structure that governed the configuration of rights and responsibilities between shareholders and managers in public corporations. More specifically, it was a legal concept that dealt with the institutional structure of how shareholders, who bore limited responsibility in proportion to their investment for the liabilities of public corporation (which could become a contractual partner under commercial law as a legal person), could control the behavior of their agents, the managers.

The issue of corporate governance has rather suddenly drawn the attention of economists in Europe and the USA, and over the past several years interdisciplinary conferences on the topic have been held by major universities and others. The Science, Technology and Industry Department of the OECD held an international conference in the winter of 1995 for the purpose of comparing the effects of corporate governance structures on economic performance in advanced nations, and the World Bank has organized several research projects on corporate governance in transition economies.

Corporate governance is now receiving worldwide attention as a major institutional issue facing market economies. This chapter deals with corporate governance in Japan, while Chapter 6 approaches the issue of corporate governance in transition economies using the results of international projects conducted at the Economic Development Institute of the World Bank. The basic perspective here is that the Anglo-American legal conceptual framework defined above can be too specific to deal with the issue of corporate governance more systematically from the perspective of comparative institutional analysis.

Though shareholders bear limited liability for the public company, they are also the legal claimants of the residual profits after payments due to the company's total liabilities have been subtracted from its total earnings. Consequently, shareholder control of managerial behavior to maximize that residual (or to minimize losses) seems on the surface to make sense. From an economic viewpoint, however, it is desirable for the firm to be managed in such a way that the "value of the firm," that is, the economic value that the firm organization produces as a whole, is maximized. The problem is that maximizing the "value of the firm" in the said sense is not necessarily consistent with maximizing the present-value sum of future residuals, in other words the stock value of the "company."

Under what circumstances will maximizing the economic value of the firm be consistent with maximizing the market value of the company for the sake of its stockholders? Assume for a moment that a perfectly competitive market exists for the services of the employees engaged in the actual production and management activities of the firm as well as for the other factors of production, and that the economic value of these factors is exogenously evaluated. Then assume that explicit employment and supply contracts can be concluded between these service providers and the firm based on its assessed market value. In this case, maximizing shareholders' returns – the residual remaining after all contractual payments, including those to debtholders, have been subtracted from the gross earnings of the firm – is the same as maximizing the value produced by the entire firm. Of course, the actual residual produced may not be maximized even under these circumstances. For example, the managers or workers may consciously or unconsciously engage in extra-contractual on-the-job perks or consumption (the moral hazard problem), or incompetent managers may either implement investment plans that do not increase returns or overlook potentially profitable investment opportunities. Mechanisms that can prevent and correct these eventualities must thus be set in place.

Ownership rights in the company include not only the right to claim the residual, but also the right to attend shareholders' meetings, to cast proxy votes, and to directly or indirectly appoint managers and sue the directors for breach of duties. Further, that bundle of rights can be sold as a divisible unit on the market. Hence the so-called "market for corporate

control rights." If investors sense that the value of the company is not
being maximized because of managerial moral hazard or incompetence,
they may be motivated to try to attain the control rights of that company
on the market. Their incentive lies in the opportunity to acquire payoffs
over and above the current value of the company, if, after obtaining corporate control rights, they can resolve the company's problems by such
means as replacing the managers. In England and the USA, the issue of
corporate governance has traditionally been approached from the perspective of how to legally secure potential corporate control for investors.
However, the issue of corporate governance has once again become a
topic of global debate because doubts have arisen as to the adequacy of
such a neoclassical approach.

Since the work of Berle and Means in the 1930s,[1] much attention has
been focused on the difficulty of managerial control by stockholders
resulting from diffused stockholdings. However, if investors possess adequate capital mobilization and information processing capabilities, the
diffusion of stockholdings itself does not necessarily mean that the stock
market loses its ability to function efficiently as a market for corporate
control. Actually, in England and the USA from the 1970s to the 1980s,
hostile takeovers were actively made through the stock market, and in
some cases through loans to bidders from the financial market, or lever-
aged buyouts (LBOs). The late 1980s, however, saw the emergence of
several phenomena that limited the efficiency of the market for corporate
control.

One of these is a takeover defense device developed by corporate management that is commonly referred to as a "poison pill." These "pills" are
prepared in advance to activate emergency financial plans for maximizing
debts and reducing shareholder assets in the event of a takeover. The ini-
tiators of a hostile takeover would thus be forced to take this "pill" against
their will. Another trend in the 1980s was for many US state legislatures,
which are responsible for legislating corporate laws, to successively revise
laws in an attempt to make company managers responsible for the fiduciary duties not only to the shareholders, but also to other stakeholders.
(Similar corporate law revisions were made in England in the early
1980s.) These revisions were originally introduced out of concern for the
social impact that a surge of hostile takeovers would have on local com-
munities. However, under the legal framework of the Anglo-American

---

[1] Adolfe Berle and Gardner Means, *The Modern Corporation and Private Property*, New
York: Macmillan, 1932.

system it gave managers a legal basis for evading legal liability for breach of stockholder interest even if they rejected a bid that would maximize the value of the company.

A third phenomenon was a rapid decrease in individual stockholdings and a concomitant increase in stockholdings by institutional investors such as pension funds and mutual funds. Because these funds invest large proportions of their assets in the stock price index to reduce risk and increase average returns, they have no incentives to monitor the management of individual companies. In any given industry, the managerial failure of A-corporation will be offset by the managerial success of B-corporation. Conversely, if mutual funds increase stockholdings to intensify the managerial monitoring of a particular company, it may become possible for that fund to be held legally responsible for its mismanagement as a parent corporate body. Consequently, with the exception of large funds like the California Public Employees' Retirement System (CalPERS) and the College Retirement Equities Fund (CREF), many institutional investors do not play an active role in corporate monitoring in spite of the fact that together they now hold more than half the stocks of listed companies.

Corporate governance has come into the spotlight in Britain and the USA because of the many problems that have arisen in regard to the efficiency of the market for corporate control, but there is substantial doubt as to whether the legal theory of Anglo-American corporate governance can be mechanically applied to situations in Japan and elsewhere as a way of solving these problems. Even under the Anglo-American system, the reality of corporate governance is a far cry from neoclassical (Walrasian) standards.

In Japan, the process of dismantling the *zaibatsu* after the war involved selling shares held by the old *zaibatsu* families and companies to the employees of those companies or to the residents of the areas in which those companies were located. Thus, when the stock market was reopened in 1949, it appeared that 70 percent of listed stocks were held by individuals. In reality, though, many of the stock purchases made by individuals were made using funds provided to those individuals by companies. As the stock market slump dragged on, many of these stocks were taken out of the hands of individuals. Because it was illegal for a company to own its own stocks or to establish a stockholding company, however, those stocks were acquired by the company's preferred stockholders, most of whom had old *zaibatsu* connections through intermediary securities firms. After the bad debts that had been created by the cancellation of governmental wartime obligations were cleared, many of the shares that were newly issued to bolster capitalization were acquired by these preferred stock-holders; hence the emergence of the phenomenon of "mutual stockhold-ing." At the end of the 1950s, holdings by financial institutions such as banks accounted for 20 percent of listed stocks, while holdings by other corporations accounted for about 15 percent of the total.

The event that first triggered mutual stockholding was a takeover attempt in 1952 by an individual investor against Yowa Fudosan (prede-cessor of Mitsubishi Estate), which owned and managed Mitsubishi real estate of the former Mitsubishi *zaibatsu* in Tokyo's Marunouchi district. As an emergency defense measure, eleven major former Mitsubishi firms joined together and devised a way to increase holdings of Yowa Fudosan stock among the group. As this episode clearly shows, the primary direct incentive for mutual stockholding under managerial leadership was the need for a defense strategy against hostile takeovers. When stock acquisi-tion by non-Japanese nationals was liberalized in the mid-1960s, the mutual stockholding rate rose even more rapidly.

Thus, the neoclassical market for corporate control was eliminated as a prevailing system in Japan. What took its place was stable stockholding by corporate stockholders centered around a main bank. A structure quite different from the neoclassical logic of corporate governance emerged. What would this mean in terms of efficiency (maximization of the firm's value)? A consideration of this issue requires that we look at corporate governance – not as a mere legalistic relationship between stockholders and managers, but in relation to the internal structure of the firm and to the financial system and labor market in which it is embedded.

ARE JAPANESE FIRMS EMPLOYEE-CONTROLLED FIRMS?

The market for corporate control does not function in Japan. Banks and other stable stockholders do not intervene in the operations of the firm as long as the financial status of the company is not critical. Though the company president (CEO) is officially elected by the board of directors, in most cases the person chosen by the retiring officer to be his successor is automatically endorsed. That successor is chosen from the pool of man-agers who have worked their way up through the ranks of the company. The general shareholders' meeting is a mere formality, and challenges to managers based on derivative suits or proxy fights by stockholders are not institutionalized. Given this, many people feel that Japanese firms are actually managed to benefit their employees.[2] Even among economists, there are many who try to explain the market behavior of Japanese firms according to the model of the worker-controlled firm. The model of worker-controlled firms is a model whose objective function is the maximization of payoffs for representative employees instead of the maximization of the stock price.

Belgian mathematical economist Jacques Drèze proved that the general equilibrium of an economy inhabited by worker-controlled firms, in which the supply and demand for all resources are equal and the income of all workers is equal, is identical with the general equilibrium of the Walrasian model.[3] This proof seemed to guarantee the universal existence of the Walrasian equilibrium regardless of differences in corporate systems. The mechanisms by which this equilibrium could be approached in the worker-controlled economy, however, were actually unrealistic. If worker incomes in one firm are higher than those in another, not only will workers from the latter firm move to the former, but the rental price of capital assets paid by the former firm will need to be raised. If employees could foresee this kind of regulating mechanism, why would they make the efforts necessary to increase the productivity of the firm?

One only has to look at the economic collapse of Yugoslavia, where worker control had been institutionalized in firms, to see that there is an enormous incentive problem where "insider control" has resulted from collusion between managers and workers. If managers do in fact act on behalf of the incumbent workers, they will distribute earnings to incumbent workers rather than make investments for future generations of workers. Also, managers who are free from the control of outside investors may try to build their own empires, and to distribute gains to workers to buy their favor. They may also waste resources on overly extravagant office buildings or on-the-job consumption. If these threats cannot be checked, the so-called "agency costs" of investors will increase, causing outside investors to refrain from entrusting their funds to managers. In other words, if the firm is financed by loans from investors, the investors may not be able to recover their funds, and if it is financed through preferred shares unaccompanied by voting rights, the insiders may cause dividends to fall through their own consumption. As a result,

[2] As a well-known example of such a contention, see James C. Abegglen and G. Stalk, Jr, *Kaisha: The Japanese Corporation*, New York: Basic Books, 1985, particularly ch. 8 ("Whose Company Is It?").

[3] Jacques Dréze, *Labour Management, Contracts and Capital Markets*, Oxford: Basil Blackwell, 1989.

worker-controlled firms cannot expect to obtain growth capital from outsiders. As will be seen in Chapter 6, the inefficiencies of insider control are a huge problem for economies in transition from communist state ownership to market economies.

This is not to imply that on-the-job consumption and lack of effort by insiders is nonexistent in Japanese firms. However, these phenomena do not exist to such a degree as to seriously reduce the efficiency of the entire economy, as they do in the former Yugoslavia and present-day Russia. Undoubtedly there must be some kind of external mechanisms at work suppressing inefficient insider behavior. In order for those external monitoring mechanisms to be effective, however, they have to be compatible with the other characteristics of Japanese firms, especially with the features of existing internal information structures. The potential for insiders (managers and other employees) to waste resources on the job and shirk their responsibilities is rooted in "information asymmetry" between insiders and outsiders. That is, outsiders cannot differentiate between the results of intentional behavior by insiders and the effects of an uncertain environment that is beyond their direct control. Consequently, attempts to control inefficient insider behavior through direct monitoring is very costly. It is more effective instead to design incentive contracts that encourage self-restraint. Insofar as the intent of these contracts is to control behavior hidden beneath the guise of uncertain environmental effects, however, they cannot be designed without considering the internal mechanisms for processing environmental information.

Because, as we have already seen, Japanese firms tend largely to endogenize the joint processing of information regarding the uncertain external environment, the incentive problems inherent in team-oriented production are rather acute. That is, because the individual's function is not clearly demarcated, their contribution to team-oriented production may not be clearly identifiable. This gives rise to the moral hazard of individuals trying to free-ride on the efforts of others, a problem that does not arise in organizations whose functional tasks are clearly delineated.

Though the efforts of each individual involved in team-oriented production are indiscernible by outsiders or managers, they are probably discernible to some degree by other members of the same team. However, not even peer monitoring and the institutionalization of standards of conduct in the workplace can solve the problem completely. Given this, is it possible to have a corporate governance structure with externally derived controls against the insider's moral hazard problem in team-oriented production? An analytical approach to this problem is covered in the next section, and the implications derived are then applied to corporate governance in Japanese firms.

TEAM-ORIENTED PRODUCTION AND "CONTINGENT GOVERNANCE"

As a purely theoretical exercise, let us assume that a firm consists of a team of workers and a manager.[4] Assume also that the output of the firm is a combined result of the effort level of each team member and an uncertain environment that cannot be directly controlled by the team. The team relies on several outside investors for the financial resources it needs to engage in production. These investors require a fixed expected rate of return for their investment (hereafter called the exogenous rate of return), but they cannot observe the actual output resulting from the individual efforts of each team member. Team members derive disutility from their labor expenditures that need to be compensated for by monetary income. The manager strives to promote reciprocal behavior between team members, but reciprocal behavior can be achieved only incompletely. That is, increased efforts by one member induce increased efforts by other members, but only imperfectly. If increased efforts by one member induced the exact same level of increased efforts by other members, the team would operate like a single individual, making it easy to control the moral hazard problem within the team. If there is no wealth constraint for team members, an exogenous rate of return may be assured for investors regardless of team output, thus making the team members the residual claimants and ensuring that they will make their best efforts. However, imperfect monitoring by either peers or managers would appear to make it impossible for efforts to be completely reciprocated. Also, if the output of the team is extremely low, the residual after subtracting the exogenous rate of return may be inadequate for supporting team members. In this case, a mechanism would be needed for guaranteeing a minimum subsistence level of income for team members.

Suppose that under these circumstances investors entrust the acquisition of their expected rate of return to an intermediary agent. Assume that this agent requires a fixed rate of compensation for performing this service, but is paid by the team requiring the investment capital. The

---

[4] The rest of this chapter draws on Masahiko Aoki, "The Contingent Governance of Teams: Analysis of Institutional Complementarity," *International Economic Review*, Vol. 35 (1994), pp. 657–76.

agent, needless to say, cannot observe the effort level of the team members, but can observe the final total output. This agent is called an "ex post monitor," meaning that the agent monitors the output realized after environmental uncertainty is resolved. The team manager concludes contracts with the ex post monitor regarding a schedule for paying investors and a schedule for compensating the ex post monitor. The latter may depend on the team's output, but, as we will see shortly, the schedule for investors, who cannot observe the team's output, must be based only on verifiable facts.

The manager also concludes a contract regarding the compensation schedule for team members that is compatible with the schedule of contractual payments to outsiders. The productivity of team members is embodied in the team; that is, it is nontransferable and individually nonportable apart from the team. If the team is disbanded, the outside income-earning potential of former team members is likely to be lower than the expected income possible on their current team. Assume that, although outside investors cannot observe the team's output, they can observe the dissolution of the team.

The manager designs a nexus of contracts among investors, the ex post monitor, and team members designed to induce from each team member a second-best level of effort that maximizes output value net of effort costs and payments to outsiders. What would such a second-best nexus of contracts look like? If we approach this problem as a constrained dynamic maximization problem, the solution will prove quite interesting.

Figure 6 divides the entire domain of possible team output at the end of each time period into three regions. From the high-end level of output there is an "insider control region," an "external intervention region," and a "liquidation region." The point that divides the first two regions is called the "control-transfer point" and the point that divides the second two regions is called the "liquidation point." The payment schedule to the various economic agents are formulated by region, as follows.

Insider control region

A fixed interest rate that exceeds the exogenous rate of return is paid to outside investors. The ex post monitor receives the same fixed rate of interest if it invests. Otherwise it receives nothing. The residual is distributed among team members. The team will survive to the next period.

External intervention region

Output control rights shift to the ex post monitor. The ex post monitor pays investors the same rate of interest as in the insider control region,

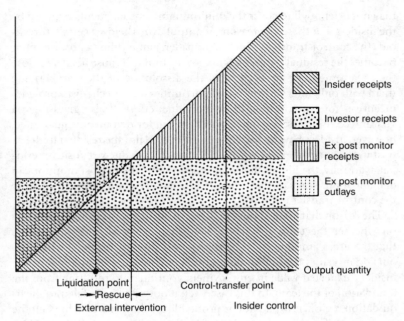

Fig. 6 Contingent governance

and pays only a fixed minimum guaranteed income to the insiders. The ex post monitor acquires the residual. The team will survive to the next period. In the areas of this region where there is not enough output after payments to investors and insiders, the residual may be negative, meaning that the ex post monitor has to rescue the team.

Liquidation region

Control rights regarding output and team survival shift to the ex post monitor. After paying the minimum guaranteed income to insiders, the ex post monitor disbands the team and pays investors a rate of interest lower than the exogenous rate of return. The ex post monitor is responsible for any output shortfalls after payment.

In the insider control region, the insiders become the residual claimants, as they are in a worker-controlled firm. However, if the insiders become residual claimants in all output regions, the moral hazard problem mentioned earlier will arise, meaning that individual workers will attempt to free-ride on the efforts of others. Also, if output is low it may not be enough to cover the minimum income payments required by the insiders. For these two reasons, if output drops below a certain threshold (the control-transfer point), an outsider, namely the ex post monitor, becomes the residual claimant. Since low output will cause insiders to lose their team membership because of the dissolution of the team, leaving them with only inferior external opportunities, this mechanism provides incentives for employees to exert individual effort. It also gives them a guaranteed minimum income. As a premium for that income guarantee, however, insiders have to forfeit their right to claim the residual to the ex post monitor at the point at which output still produces a positive residual. Naturally, the higher the compensation that the ex post monitor can demand for its services, that is, the greater its bargaining power, the higher the control-transfer point will be.

The reason that interest rates paid to outside investors differ depending on whether the team survives or is disbanded is as follows. Suppose that the gross amount saved by the ex post monitor in the payment to outside investors through liquidation is exactly equal to the loss of the insiders' expected value of employment continuation resulting from the liquidation of the team. In this case, even if output were to fall into the liquidation region, it would not be profitable for the insiders to buy out the ex post monitor to avoid liquidation. Economically speaking, the liquidation is said to be "renegotiation-proof." The ex post monitor's commitment to liquidation becomes credible so that the incentive effect of the nexus of contracts will be guaranteed. This also, however, produces an incentive for the ex post monitor to liquidate the team rather than rescue it in the lower end of the external intervention region, because the monitor will minimize its losses by doing so. The problem of how to control this adverse incentive of the ex post monitor will be addressed in the next chapter.

CONTINGENT GOVERNANCE AND THE MAIN BANK

The optimal nexus of contracts specified above defines a "contingent governance" structure in team-oriented production which transfers decision-making authority regarding both the distribution of output residual and the continuation of the team between insiders and outsiders contingent upon final output. Readers have probably already surmised that a governance structure defined in this way bears a striking resemblance to the relationship between Japanese firms and their main banks until the mid-1970s.[5] Many households chose to receive a stable deposit rate through their bank account as their primary means of holding their financial assets. The banks met the flourishing demand for corporate loans through joint financing, but the main bank of the borrowing firm was entrusted with maintaining the expected rate of return. As long as the firm remained in excellent financial health, its bargaining power vis-à-vis the main bank was strong, its interest payments were relatively low, and the bank could not intervene in the details of the firm's management. However, if the financial state of the firm became less than excellent but better than distressed, the main bank was able to extract higher revenues from it through such measures as requiring the firm to hold higher compensating balances. The main bank was also able to reap special benefits from managing the firm's major settlement accounts and providing other financial services, as well as by offering its own employees career opportunities by sending them into the firm as managing directors.

Once a financed firm encountered financial difficulties, however, it was understood that the main bank would bear the responsibility for the governance of the firm. If it were deemed that the firm's financial difficulties were only temporary, or that restructuring was possible, the main bank would take responsibility for paying the costs necessary for bailing out the firm and guaranteeing the employment of its core employees. The main bank also had to guarantee the payment of debts to other banks. If restructuring was not possible, however, the main bank would take measures to either liquidate the firm or merge it with another firm. Even in this case, the main bank was often responsible for the re-employment of terminated employees, who were penalized for the failure of the firm by being given less advantageous re-employment terms. Other banks were also made to pay part of the liquidation costs. The main bank did not make it a rule to always bail out troubled firms.

Corporate governance in Japanese firms until the mid-1970s featured a contingent governance structure in which the main bank played the role of the ex post monitor. (The changes that occurred in this structure later are discussed in the following section.) How did this structure differ from a corporate governance structure operating through a market for corporate control? Even in the market, takeover attempts depended on the financial status of the firm; they were not of any economic gain and thus

---

[5] For the main bank relationships of the Japanese firm, see various chapters of Masahiko Aoki and Hugh Patrick (eds.), *The Japanese Main Bank System: Its Relevance to Developing and Transforming Economies*, Oxford and New York: Oxford University Press, 1994, particularly chs. 1, 4, and 6.

would not be initiated as long as the market value of the company (the stock price) did not fall below its potential level. However, even if the financial status of the firm was good, it was not unusual for the board of directors to select an outsider as CEO. Also, if a firm took a turn for the worse, it took some time before the situation came to the attention of a takeover bidder. In the event of a takeover, there was no way to guarantee the re-employment of the workers. Actually, Andrei Shleifer and Lawrence Summers have given statistical evidence that a significant portion of the increases in company value achieved through takeovers in the USA in the 1980s were a result of breaching tacit contracts between workers and former managers.[6] There is no way to conclude an employment contract that specifies the terms of restructuring, as it is not known ahead of time who will initiate and implement a takeover.

Under contingent governance by a main bank, by contrast, the matter of who will gain control rights in the event of the firm's financial decline is well understood in advance. Consequently, the main bank is not likely to shirk its duty to continuously monitor the firm's financial status, because any delay in learning about financial problems may result in increased restructuring or liquidation costs, which are borne solely by the main bank. As we will see in the next chapter, if the appropriate incentives are provided to the main bank, its commitment to contingent rescue or liquidation will be credible. As a result, the main bank may not only be able to preserve team-oriented production assets during temporary difficulties, but may also be able to control the incentive problems inherent in team-oriented production. Contingent governance by a main bank may be the complementary framework for Japanese companies whose internal organization schemes are based on assimilated information architecture.

An interesting implication of contingent governance can be derived from a comparative statics analysis of the second-best nexus of contracts. To the extent that the expected re-employment value of the members of a team that has been disbanded decreases, the liquidation point in the second-best contract rises, as does the effort level of the team members (approaching the first-best contract). That is, the poorer the re-employment market, the stronger the incentive effects of contingent governance. Within the context of the main bank system, we can say,

---

[6] Andrei Shleifer and Lawrence Summers, "Breach of Trust in Hostile Takeovers," in Alan J. Auerbach (ed.), *Corporate Takeovers: Causes and Consequence*, Chicago: University of Chicago Press, 1988, pp. 33–67.

therefore, that institutional complementarity exists between the imperfect labor market and the contingent control of the main bank with regard to the incentive effects of team-oriented production. It goes without saying that the Japanese re-employment market for workers terminated from financially distressed firms is as imperfect as the market for corporate control is absent. This situation stands in stark contrast to corporate governance through the market for corporate control whose efficiency is assured by the existence of a perfectly competitive labor market.

CAPITAL ACCUMULATION OF THE FIRM AND PHASES IN THE RELATIVE BARGAINING POWER OF INSIDERS AND OUTSIDERS

The effectiveness of corporate governance seen in the last section will change depending on the bargaining power relationship between the firm and the ex post monitor (the main bank), a relationship that rests on the financial viability of the firm and the availability of non-bank financing options. Let us call the output level at which the probability of output is maximized in the second-best contract the "maximum likelihood output." Given this definition, the relationship between the firm and the ex post monitor (the main bank) can be classified into the following three developmental phases. This analysis will also be useful later (Chapter 6) in discussing issues of corporate governance in transition economies.

Quasi-soft budget constraint
The productivity of production teams is especially low. However, since the compensation demanded by the ex post monitor is also low, the ex post monitor does not insist on claiming its rights to the residual at the maximum likelihood output. Also, there is a high probability that the ex post monitor will have to compensate for output shortfalls.

Strong external control
The ex post monitor has strong bargaining power relative to the production teams, and becomes the residual claimant at the maximum likelihood output.

Weak external control
The ex post monitor has weak bargaining power relative to the production teams, and the insiders become the residual claimants at the maximum likelihood output.

In each of these three phases, how will the second-best contract react to changes in the bargaining power relationship between the production teams and the ex post monitor, or to team productivity increases? A comparative statics analysis reveals the following.

In the first phase, the residual claimed by the ex post monitor can increase only if the insiders' incentives are weakened. Therefore, the ex post monitor should not demand a very high level of compensation for incentives for insiders to be created in this phase. However, it will be best if the control-transfer point and the liquidation point rise accordingly as the productivity of the production team rises, thereby increasing the incentives for team members as well.

In the second phase, the weakening (or strengthening) of the ex post monitor's rights to claim the residual, as well as increases in team productivity, strengthen (or weaken) the incentive effects of contingent governance on insiders. This is because the margin of residual available to each team member increases (or decreases). In the third phase, by contrast, the weakening of the ex post monitor's bargaining power weakens the incentive effects of corporate governance on insiders. Because the insider control region will expand greatly in this case, the possibility of penalization by a transfer of control to the ex post monitor decreases, and opportunities for insiders to free-ride on each other increase. However, even in this phase, the incentive effects of corporate governance are strengthened by the production team's increased productivity.

The results of this comparative statics analysis help explain the transitions in firm–main bank relations in Japan. After the Second World War, the capital bases of firms were weakened by rising inflation and the cancellation of governmental wartime obligations. Consequently, banks could not claim the residual from firms, as in the first phase. Rather, they had to soften their budgets to bail out firms in times of financial crisis. The bank's cooperative attitude may have provided the firm with an incentive to make efforts to acquire the payoffs made possible by financial viability.

Through the rebirth of bank-centered corporate groups in the 1950s, banks were able to increase their bargaining power relative to firms that were seeking large amounts of capital for high growth. In this phase, the firm's desire to limit excessive bank intervention by accumulating its own capital provided the firm's insiders with strong incentives. As a result of their efforts, the internal accumulation of capital resulted in the initiation of a virtuous cycle of growth. Main-bank-oriented contingent governance functioned as a whole most effectively during this time.

However, because of the slowdown in the growth rate and declining business efforts by firms that occurred around 1975, drastic changes began to take place in the dominant position of banks vis-à-vis firms. After that point, banks were no longer in a position to demand the main bank rent through such measures as requiring the firm to hold compensating balances. In this situation, analogous to the third phase, the incentive effects of contingent governance by a main bank declined the more the bargaining power of firms was strengthened by the firms' use of external financing sources, such as the Eurobond market.

Even now that the bubble has burst, however, it is not altogether clear whether contingent governance, which integrated insurance and incentive functions, has finally met its demise. Japanese firms still retain aspects of team-oriented production, and theoretically the market for corporate control cannot offer complementary monitoring functions over those firms. Also, as we saw earlier, the functions of the market for corporate control are retreating even in the Anglo-American system. So can contingent governance be reformed in some way? Can banks continue to play the same role as before in this kind of governance structure? Or is it possible to reconstruct contingent governance such that banks do not play an active role? We will return to these questions in Chapter 7 after analyzing the bank incentive structure that sustained the main bank system.

The Main Bank System and Government Regulations

THREE STAGES OF CORPORATE MONITORING

The last chapter examined one aspect of the Japanese main bank system from the viewpoint of the corporate governance of firms. The role of the main bank was to provide external verification of the financial state of the firm and to invoke certain control rights depending on that state. However, those activities naturally involve some costs to the main bank. What kind of incentives would the main bank have to carry out those control activities that would seem theoretically optimal? Could it develop the abilities needed to engage in those activities? Perhaps the nature of the overall financial system in which firms and banks are embedded, as well as the regulatory framework that governs them, are relevant for answering these questions. However, the regulatory framework cannot be arbitrarily and exogenously designed by the government: its effectiveness changes as the relationship between firms and various financial institutions, including banks, evolve. This chapter takes a broad perspective that includes the dimension of corporate governance to address questions of how the comparative features of the main bank system should be understood, what the nature of the regulatory framework supporting that system was, and how its effectiveness has changed as the economy has moved through its various phases.

Transactions involving investible funds between investors (suppliers of funds in the form of equity or credit) and a firm undertaking a business project entail a substantial degree of information asymmetry and imperfection. First, investors may not be as well informed as the firm regarding the technological and marketing opportunities that define the outcome of a project (the adverse selection or "hidden information" problem). Second, managers of the firm themselves may not necessarily be in an advantageous position with regard to information if the financial returns of the project depend upon coordinated undertakings of complementary projects by other firms (the coordination problem). Third, a manager's promise to use the funds for a certain profitable purpose may not be fulfilled because of manager (or worker) incompetence or morally hazardous behavior hidden behind the guise of uncontrollable random events (the moral hazard or "hidden action" problem).

Coping with these problems requires mechanisms for assessing the creditworthiness of proposed projects, tracking the use of funds, and distinguishing misuse from temporary bad luck, as well as a commitment to penalizing misuse as a safeguard against future misuse (the commitment problem). Thus, the supply of financial resources requires a substantial degree of concomitant information collection – monitoring – by investors before and after the actual investment, as well as their participation in controlling the firm. Corporate monitoring and control is only possible, however, with special expertise, concentrated resources, and a sufficiently broad scope in terms of cross-industrial coverage as well as time horizon. In capitalist economies a variety of financial intermediaries and agents specializing in corporate monitoring and control have emerged. A particular set of institutional arrangements webbed by such institutions evolves for each economy. These are conditioned partly by the existing regulatory framework, partly by historical conditions, and partly as a response to the prevailing and emergent organizational, technological, and risk taking attributes of the economy. This chapter is concerned with the structure that has emerged in the Japanese economy, while the following chapter looks at corporate governance structures in the context of transition economies.

The word "monitor" is used to mean "to check or observe" and then "to regulate" on the basis of the information collected. In applying the term "monitor" to the actions taken by the suppliers of funds (or their agents) toward firms to overcome the problems associated with information asymmetry and imperfection, we must make a conceptual differentiation between three kinds of monitoring. The primary distinction is the timing of the monitoring action vis-à-vis the transfer of funds from the investor to the firm.

The first stage of monitoring, ex ante, refers to the investor's assessment of the creditworthiness of investment projects proposed by firms and their screening. Generally this type of monitoring is considered economically valuable, as it can reduce the problem of adverse selection and prevent coordination failures between complementary investment projects. For example, the profitability of a steel plant is affected by the availability of power, which may in turn be crucially affected by the construction of a new dam if the level of capital accumulation in the electric power industry is relatively low. Investors must thus be able to collect a broad range of cross-industrial information on investment projects to perform adequate ex ante monitoring.

The second stage, interim monitoring, refers to the stage in which investors consistently check up on the operations of the firm, after funds have been committed, to prevent the moral hazard problem. The third stage of monitoring, ex post, refers to the verification of the performance outcome (the financial state) of the firm, the determination of the long-run viability of the firm in the case of financial distress, and the use of that information for possible corrective or punitive action. The role of the ex post monitor in contingent governance, as discussed in the previous chapter, corresponds to this stage of monitoring. If investors (or their agents) make a credible commitment to punish poor performance, management will be careful to avoid ex ante information processing and interim behavior that might result in a poor outcome. Thus, a credible commitment to ex post monitoring serves as a mechanism to control the adverse selection and moral hazard problems.

The distinctions between the three stages of monitoring should be regarded as merely conceptual; in practice they are inextricably inter-twined. For example, if the relationship between the investor and the firm are repeatable over time, the information gained from the interim monitoring of a previous investment may be used in decisions regarding new financing. Nonetheless, the conceptual distinction is quite useful for comparing the structure and performance of different financial systems.

The monitoring of different stages may be delegated to various financial intermediaries and agents that specialize in the functions of each stage in order to reduce information costs and the costs of duplicate monitoring. Institutional arrangements for such intermediaries may differ across economies, however. Under the Anglo-American system, for example, ex ante monitoring is performed by investment banks acting as underwriters for large established firms, by venture capital firms for entrepreneurial start-up firms, by commercial banks for conventional smaller firms, and so on. Rating companies may be considered to be engaged in interim monitoring in that they keep track of the changing financial state of the firm, but they also can be considered an important ex ante monitoring agent in the securities-based financial system insofar as their evaluation affects the capacity of firms to raise new funds from capital markets. Interim monitoring of management may be most directly performed by the board of directors, which in turn is subject to direct and indirect pressure from major stockholders as well as a variety of funds managers, market arbitrageurs, and others. The court-led bankruptcy procedure constitutes an important ex post control device in any financial system. However, the institutionalization of the market for corporate control may be regarded as the most distinctive ex post monitoring device of the Anglo-American system as it is unparalleled elsewhere.

In contrast to the highly decentralized Anglo-American system, in which the three stages of monitoring are entrusted to separate specialized intermediaries, the Japanese main bank system in its heyday (from the 1950s to the mid 1970s) was characterized as a system in which the three stages of monitoring were highly integrated and exclusively delegated to the main bank of the firm.

EXCLUSIVE DELEGATION OF INTEGRATED MONITORING TO THE MAIN BANK

In the early part of Japan's high growth period, the coordination of information exchange and expectation formation by public institutions such as the Council of Coordinating Electric Energy Source Development and the Industrial Funding Division of the Industrial Structure Council, as well as the leadership of the Japan Development Bank and the Industrial Bank of Japan in making lending decisions, provided useful guidelines for the lending decisions of city banks. Over the course of the high growth period, however, the ex ante monitoring function changed. Main banks accounted for an average of approximately 20 percent of a firm's loans, with the remainder being divided between other city banks, long-term credit banks, local banks, trust banks, insurance companies, and agricultural cooperative financial institutions. However, the formation of a de facto loan consortium was made possible only with the initial lead decision by the main bank to extend a certain critical portion of the required investment funds. Other financial institutions, with the exception of long-term credit banks, relied on the main bank's credit analysis rather than developing their own monitoring capabilities. In other words, the ex ante monitoring function was implicitly delegated to the main bank by the other institutions.

The ability of the main bank to assume such ex ante responsibility was derived from the even greater role of the main bank in interim and ex post monitoring. When the Japanese economy was still in the stages of technological catch-up, the assessment of managerial and organizational ability of an investing firm to absorb and refine engineering know-how developed abroad was a more important component of ex ante monitoring than the assessment of the commercial and engineering value of an emergent technology, per se. The engineering assessments of imported technologies for large-scale projects were often delegated to the Japan Development Bank and the Industrial Bank of Japan, which were impartial to any financial *keiretsu* grouping, and had developed the necessary engineering and credit analysis capabilities. The city banks were, however, well equipped to assess the organizational and managerial ability of firms belonging to their own *keiretsu* groupings.

The main bank extended a far larger share of short-term loans to its customers, and managed their major payment settlement accounts. This information gathering capability amounted to an ability to partially open the books of the firm. Such interim monitoring opportunities provided city banks with private information useful for judging the organizational and managerial capabilities of borrowing firms. The exclusive role of the main bank in ex post monitoring was already touched upon in the previous chapter. The unwritten but well observed code dictated that when a firm fell into a financially depressed state it was the responsibility of the main bank to resolve the problem by taking the initiative to either rescue or restructure the firm.

In the USA the doctrine of "equitable subordination" makes claims by lenders involved in the business of troubled firms subordinate to other claims in the eventuality of bankruptcy. This rule deters commercial banks in the Anglo-American system from being actively involved in rescuing or restructuring failing firms.[1] Although a similar rule appears to have been imposed de facto in the Japanese system, within the context of the exclusive delegation of integrated monitoring, it seems to have motivated the main banks to perform earnest interim and ex ante monitoring. Main banks needed to prevent client firms from undertaking projects that might place more than the amount of their own lending at risk, and they needed to closely monitor the business affairs of borrowing firms to facilitate the earliest possible detection of potential problems. This motivation encouraged other lenders to delegate ex ante monitoring to the main bank.

Another possible effect of integrated monitoring was that it may have reduced incentives for the borrowing firm to conceal or misrepresent information to the main bank, particularly at the interim stage. When the

[1] Mark Ramseyer, "Explicit Reason for Implicit Contracts: The Legal Logic to the Japanese Main Bank System," in M. Aoki and H. Patrick (eds.), *The Japanese Main Bank System*, pp. 231–57.

main bank took control of a firm under the contingent governance scheme, it had the option of imposing weak or heavy penalties on management, depending on the magnitude of the problem. Concealing potential problems, evading the intervention of the main bank, and putting off problems may have resulted in harsher penalties by the main bank at later stages. In order to elicit the main bank's "gentler" terms of rescue, management was obliged to be honest. By concentrating its settlement accounts and other banking business on the main bank, management was effectively submitting itself to the bank's interim monitoring. Voluntary disclosure by the firm reduced not only interim information gathering costs for the main bank, but the costs of implementing ex post problem solving measures as well.

An additional effect of exclusive integrated monitoring by the main bank was that it expanded the range of potential actions the main bank could implement ex post. As has already been shown, the main bank's feasible options for dealing with ailing firms ranged from liquidation to reorganization, bank-managed restructuring, and simple loan rescheduling. However, the underwriters and initial holders of bonds could not commit themselves ex ante to such a broad range of options because, facing liquid secondary markets, they could sell their claims at any time, thereby inducing a change in the identity of maturity date holders. Consequently, when a debt could not be paid, the only option available for bondholders could be the one formally stipulated by legal bankruptcy procedures. Under the exclusive loan relationship observed in the Japanese economy in the 1920s, on the other hand, it became difficult for the bank to refuse to rescue financially distressed partner firms. If lending were diversified, however, as it was under the main bank system, the viable options available to the main bank would have included both liquidation and rescue, depending on the specific circumstances of the case.

It has often been contended that the relationship between the main bank and the firm is a reciprocal long-term commitment, but an unconditional commitment to a long-term relationship would dilute the incentives of the firm's employees to exert any effort. Integrated monitoring would be more appropriately characterized as a mechanism that expands the range of actions that can be implemented by the main bank ex post. Contingent governance theory shows that this expansion of the range of options has positive incentive effects on team-oriented firms.

The implications of this flexibility are not altogether clear a priori, however. On the one hand, it may have contributed to the preservation of valuable managerial and organizational resources of viable firms during periods of temporary distress; on the other hand, it may have facilitated "soft budgeting" by the main banks (ex post relaxation of budgetary constraints in inefficient firms). Only future empirical studies will determine which was the final outcome.

POSSIBILITY OF A MAIN BANK EQUILIBRIUM

The previous chapter discussed the incentive effects on firms subject to main bank monitoring. This section examines the theoretical incentives for the main bank to perform the exclusively delegated integrated monitoring function. What motivated the main bank to undertake ex ante and interim monitoring? How was the main bank motivated to rescue failing firms when the rescue cost appeared to exceed the default value of its own credit? Why did the main bank not default on its obligation to rescue and choose instead to liquidate financially depressed firms more frequently? This section tries to explain that a kind of rent played an important role in preserving the main bank's commitment to the contingency contract, especially its commitment to rescue temporarily distressed firms.

Suppose that the economic activities of firms and banks are conducted at discrete time intervals. Suppose a firm's output at the end of a period is possible at only three levels – high, (temporarily) low, or critical – as a result of the combined effects of firm effort and uncontrollable circumstances. Suppose also that the probability distribution over these levels depends on whether or not the main bank conducts interim monitoring of the firm's efforts during the term. If it does, the probability of high output becomes higher and that of critical output becomes lower. If the output level at the end of a term is high, the main bank is able to extract a certain level of premium over the normal rate of financial returns in the market (the main bank rent). If the output level is low, the main bank has the option of liquidating the firm with a negative premium (equal to the difference between the collateral value and the default value of credit), or rescuing it and incurring the costs of meeting the claims of other creditors. If the output level is critical, the main bank has the same options but with an even lower rate of return or higher costs.

If the firm is not liquidated, the main bank relationship will continue into the next period, when the main bank will make a new decision regarding whether or not to monitor. Suppose, however, that when firms in the critical output state are rescued they shirk in future periods, believing that the main bank will never punish them. In this case, it is no longer in the main bank's interest to monitor such firms. That is, once the main bank rescues a firm in the critical output state, it is privately optimal for it not to subsequently monitor that firm.

If the expected increase in the output of a firm due to monitoring during the period exceeds the monitoring costs, it is socially optimal to rescue firms with temporarily low output and to continue to monitor them in subsequent periods. However, rescuing low-output firms may be privately costlier to the main bank, as it has to guarantee other creditors' claims. Since the true output level is not observable to anyone other than the main bank to which ex post monitoring is delegated, the main bank may be motivated for its own purposes to liquidate even temporarily low output firms, even though such behavior is socially suboptimal.

To counteract such behavior, let us suppose that penalties – reductions of main bank rents – are imposed indiscriminately on main banks that liquidate firms, regardless of the externally nonobservable output. We will later examine how such penalties are imposed. If penalties are sufficiently high, the main bank will not liquidate firms with low output. The problem with this scheme, however, is that if penalties are too high, the main bank may be motivated to rescue firms at the critical low output level at which they should be liquidated. Thus, liquidation penalties should be neither too high nor too low. Therefore, the following proposition holds:

There is a range of liquidation penalties (rents) that are neither too high nor too low, under which the main bank always liquidates firms at the critically low output level, but rescues firms at the temporary low output level and continues to maintain its main bank relationship with them in the next period. The main bank will continue to perform interim monitoring of the rescued firms, and the rescued firms will not shirk.

If the prescribed penalties can be imposed, integrated monitoring within the period or ex post monitoring becomes incentive-compatible for the main bank, even if the true output level of the firm is neither observable nor verifiable by other creditors, and the "main bank equilibrium" (as the subgame-perfect equilibrium of the repeated game) at which the firm exerts the highest level of effort becomes sustainable. However, if the main bank rent is not sufficiently high, or if the liquidation penalties are too low, then another "low equilibrium" may emerge at which banks do not perform interim monitoring and firms shirk as a consequence. Conversely, excessively high main bank rent and excessively high penalties will result in another low equilibrium at which banks do not liquidate firms at the critical low output level and firms shirk as a result.

This suggests that different equilibria will result depending on the level of exogenously determined rents; but can the level of rents at which the main bank equilibrium would be possible be maintained if free entry to the banking industry is possible? Can banks capable of performing main bank monitoring distinguish themselves from banks that do not have those monitoring capabilities, and can they extract sufficient main bank rents (minus monitoring and rescue costs) by committing to contingent governance? Serdar Dinç has analyzed this problem.[2]

Dinç's model has two types of firms and two types of banks. Both types of firm survive for only two production periods. The L-firm in this model continuously undertakes only low-risk/low-return projects that last only one period, while the H-firm can also undertake projects with high uncertainty that extend over two periods. If the latter type of project is selected, at the end of the first period it becomes certain that output at the end of the second period will be either high, moderately low, or critically low. Which of these outputs will occur is determined stochastically. (Thus, there is no moral hazard problem for the firm.) If a firm's final output is high, the bank that financed that firm can claim a portion of the firm's earnings as rent, but if output is critically low, it would be socially optimal for the bank to liquidate the firm immediately at the end of the first period. However, suppose that private benefits accruable to the moderately low output firm from rescue can be greater than the rescue costs of the bank. Then the socially optimal choice for dealing with a firm with a moderately low (but not critical) level of output would be for the bank, as stated above, to rescue the firm at its own private expense. However, when the firm is in either of the two low-level output positions, it is impossible for the bank to discern whether it is moderately or critically low without expending the monitoring costs involved in performing the monitoring function. There are two kinds of bank: C (competent)-banks, whose monitoring costs are relatively low and which are thus able to more accurately assess a firm's financial state at the end of the first period, and I (incompetent)-banks, whose monitoring costs are relatively high and which are thus relatively less able to discern between moderately and critically low output situations. The type of firm being dealt with can be determined through ex ante monitoring, but the type of bank will

[2] Serdar Dinç, "Bank Competition, Relationship Banking and the Path Dependence," Ph.D. dissertation, Stanford University, 1996. Also see his "Bank Reputation, Bank Commitment and the Effects of the Competition in Credit Markets," *Review of Financial Studies*, forthcoming.

be revealed only by the bank's history of rescue activities, as will be shown below.

In this model, if H-firms are not assured of being rescued by a bank if their output levels fall, they have no incentive to undertake high-risk/high-return projects that extend over two periods. Since the firm will survive for only two periods or will switch its bank after two periods, the bank will not be able to extract any direct returns from rescuing the firm. However, if the bank can establish a reputation for its commitment to rescue over the long term, it will be able to attract H-firms as clients, and will have reason to believe that it will be able to extract some rents in the future. If the bank is an I-bank, however, it will either not engage in rescue operations or will engage in rescue operations only in cases where rescue is known to be viable, because it is too costly to indiscriminately rescue ailing firms based on incomplete information. In this case, the frequency of a bank's rescue operations will make it clear over time what type of bank the bank is, and I-banks that imitate C-banks will gradually be eliminated. Also, C-banks with high monitoring capacities may sink reputation capital in the form of bailing out moderately low-output H-firms in the first period in an attempt to deter the entry of I-banks.

Does this model also suggest the possibility of achieving a main bank equilibrium at which C-banks committed to rescuing firms will expel I-banks, and at which H-firms undertake high-risk/high-return long-term projects? The answer, as before, is that if the main bank rent is within an intermediate range, and if the number of C-banks and H-firms is relatively high, equilibrium is possible. If the rent is too high, there will be no incentive for the H-firm to undertake high-risk/high-return projects. If the rent is too low, there will be no incentive for the C-bank to rescue moderately low-output H-firms in the first period. A relatively high number of C-banks and H-firms is needed to increase the probability for matching that will make it possible to achieve the main bank equilibrium. The level of rents is exogenously given in this model, but it can be regarded as endogenously determined by bidding between C-banks and I-banks. At an equilibrium where a positive rent is established, even if the I-banks compete for lower levels of rent against C-banks, in the end it will be the I-banks that suffer a loss.

The Dinc model suggests that main bank rents are acquired wholly from the earnings of the better firms. It is also possible, however, for rents to be transferred from depositors to banks. If the bank guarantees the safety of assets, depositors may be willing to pay the bank an insurance premium, just like the firm pays rents to the bank on the condition of its commitment to rescue. As Joseph Stiglitz and Andrew Weiss have shown, the determination of the interest rate through bidding may result in the adverse selection of a high-risk borrower that has no incentive to service its debts and will default on its loans.[3]

THE REGULATORY FRAMEWORK AND MAIN BANK RENT

The discussion thus far suggests four potential social benefits of the main bank system:

1. Contingent intervention by the main bank, made possible by the main bank's integration of the three stages of monitoring, may provide a complementary external disciplinary mechanism for team-oriented production.
2. The exclusive delegation of corporate monitoring to the main bank prevents the social costs of duplicate ex ante and interim monitoring if the information to be processed is relatively standardized.
3. Main bank rescue operations may prevent the premature liquidation of temporarily depressed, but potentially productive, firms.
4. Entrapment at a low equilibrium, arising from the failure to coordinate high-risk/high-return investment projects may be avoided.

Realizing these benefits, however, is contingent upon the implementation of integrated monitoring and requires that incentive rents be available for the main bank. The previous section suggested two theoretical possibilities for rent formation: (i) in some cases a positive rent is maintained by exogenous factors, and (ii) in others it is endogenized through competition among banks that possess monitoring capabilities to invest in establishing their reputations. Later we will see that these two are not always mutually exclusive, but first let us look at the role played by the regulations pertaining to the formation of rents. The regulatory framework for the main bank system established by the Ministry of Finance and the Bank of Japan rested on the following four premises:

1. Keep the deposit interest rate low, but maintain a positive real rate by simultaneously controlling the rate of inflation (financial restraint).

---

[3] Joseph Stiglitz and Andrew Weiss, "Credit Rationing in Markets with Imperfect Information," *American Economic Review*, Vol. 71 (1981), pp. 393–410.

2. Restrict bond issuance to privileged firms, and restrain the development of the secondary bond market.
3. Restrict new entry to the banking industry, especially to the city bank category, as city banks can become the main banks of large firms.
4. Institute a performance-based reward/penalty system for banks, such as branch licensing, the dispatch of ex-bureaucrats as executives, etc.

Under premises 1 and 2, the competitiveness of each bank is conditioned on its ability to acquire deposits, which in turn is affected by the number and location of its branches, as well as the number, size, and earning power of the corporate clients whose settlement accounts it manages. Suppose the distribution of deposits at the regulated deposit rate among banks is determined by branch-licensing (premiss 4) and banks' historical connections with client firms (ignoring the fierce competition for deposits among banks). Suppose further that, on the basis of premisses 2 and 3, the normal lending rate is anchored to the deposit rate with a normal profit margin (ignoring any lending rate differentiation). This then, together with the repression of the deposit rate (premiss 1), affords main banks an opportunity to accrue rents by selecting good client firms.

When a firm becomes financially depressed, its main bank can liquidate it. However, if a particular main bank resorts to liquidation too frequently, its reputation as a responsible monitor will be damaged. As a result: (*a*) depositors may change banks because of concerns over the security of their deposits; (*b*) other financial institutions may be reluctant to participate in joint financing consortia for that bank's customers because the bank's lending decisions no longer signal the creditworthiness of borrowers; (*c*) that bank's other client firms may switch their main bank relationships for fear of losing insurance in adversity and losing access to credit from other lenders; and (*d*) regulatory authorities concerned about the social consequences of bankruptcy, such as partial or total loss of confidence in the financial system, may directly penalize banks that liquidate too frequently by dispatching managers to those banks or restricting their branch licensing.

This suggests that the costs for a main bank to abandon a client firm that has fallen into financial distress extend beyond the mere loss of its irrecoverable debts. However, because main banks naturally take these possibilities into consideration when dealing with depressed firms, such penalties are not actually often observed. The outcome of equilibrium will be that, because of the expectation of severe penalties, banks select

actions that maintain their reputations, and consequently choose to liquidate large and medium-sized firms only infrequently.

Now we will take up a theoretical concept mentioned in the previous
section and examine the role of banking industry entrance regulations
(premiss 3) and bond market repression (premiss 2) in the formation and
maintenance of the main bank system.

Stated in terms of the Dinç model, if the relative number of I-banks
increases due to free entry, the probability that borrowers, who cannot
distinguish between C-banks and I-banks, will be liquidated during temporary financial downturns will increase. In this situation, even if the
long-term project of an H-firm is technologically feasible, it will entail a
great deal of economic risk. As a result, even H-firms will select short-
term, low-risk projects. Conversely, if the probability that a C-bank can
lend to an H-firm decreases, the gains that can be earned by the C-bank
will be low even if the level of expected rent per H-firm is fairly high. Consequently, if the number of H-firms is posited as a given, the absolute
number of C-banks will have to be small in order for the main bank equilibrium to be achieved. Thus, for a main bank system to arise from a
matching of firms and banks mutually committed to a long-term relationship, the number of banks must be limited. Especially when monitoring capabilities are not yet fully developed in all banks, the mechanism by
which main banks are formed and their reputations firmly established
can be accelerated by exogenously identifying the small number of C-
bank candidates and providing them with incentives for learning the
behaviors of C-banks in the Dinç model.

The Japanese banking system of the 1920s included more than two
thousand banks, none of which had yet developed into modern banks
committed to integrated monitoring. Not even the *zaibatsu* banks
financed firms (except for trading companies) within the same *zaibatsu*
group. This banking rivalry offered no incentives for either banks or firms
to pursue a main bank relationship. As a result of government merger and
acquisition promotion policies from the 1930s to the end of the war
period, however, the number of rival banks dropped to sixty-five. During
the war period, these banks participated in joint financing consortia led
by the Industrial Bank of Japan and strengthened their relationships with
designated firms under the Designated Financial System for Munitions
Loans, but they did not go so far as to carry out the exclusive, integrated
monitoring function of a main bank. Such capabilities first appeared in
the high growth period that began in the 1950s, and were motivated by
rents produced from the regulatory framework discussed above. That is,

the city banks that later evolved into the main banks of large firms were motivated to develop and apply integrated monitoring capabilities in return for the acquisition of regulatory rents, but were not initially in a position of being able to acquire rents through the autonomous development of monitoring capabilities. Even after the establishment of the main bank system, institutionalizing limits on the total number of banks and formalizing distinctions between the position of city and local bank seemed to function as a framework for selecting a "particular" main bank equilibrium from among the many equilibria possible and for maintaining that equilibrium at a low social cost.

If liquidation penalties were imposed exclusively as in (b) and (c) above, the resulting equilibrium might have approached the second-best contingent governance determined by the relative bargaining power of the main bank and the firm because there would be no incentives to rescue socially inefficient firms. However, if banks believed that the politico-economic mechanism of (d) was functioning, they might have tended to engage in "soft budgeting," or to rescue socially inefficient firms to avoid the large stigma associated with creating unemployment. This point needs to be verified by empirical research.

Once a main bank system is set in place, main bank relationships may never be completely eliminated even if rents decrease or entry regulations are relaxed. Rents may decrease if an alternative financial system, such as the bond market, is developed. For a new C-bank to establish its reputation as a main bank, it may have to distinguish itself from an I-bank not only by making a commitment to rescue firms facing temporary hardship, but also by paying the costs of lowering initial interest rates for H-firms to attract them as customers. For this to be profitable, however, the final expected rent has to be high. Consequently, the likelihood of a rent decrease after the establishment of the main bank system may serve as a barrier to entry. Because the existing main banks have already paid the price of establishing a reputation for themselves, they can continue to survive even if the rents are decreased by competition from bond markets. This is a type of path dependence. If there is a severe decrease in rents, however, even established main banks will not be able to survive.

DECLINING MONITORING CAPABILITIES OF BANKS IN A MARKET ENVIRONMENT

The regulatory framework outlined in the last section has undergone some irreversible changes since the mid 1970s. In the late 1970s two pillars of the regulatory framework, the regulation of interest rates and bond issue requirements, were gradually eliminated. Firms have come to rely increasingly on bond issues in the Eurobond market, while noncompetitive rent opportunities for banks through interest rate regulation have decreased drastically. Through the 1980s, however, main banks were able to benefit from their clients' Eurobond issues by acting as bond issuance managers through foreign subsidiaries and earning income from foreign exchange transactions and processing fees. These benefits may be interpreted as a form of main bank rent that they could acquire because of the reputations these banks had made for themselves. Their gains from these services were probably lower than they were during the golden age of the main bank system, reflecting the strong relative bargaining power of firms that had found alternative fund raising sources. However, to the extent that the decline in rents did not occur suddenly, it served to ensure the possibility that established main banks could survive even without explicit regulations restricting new entrants.

Still, entrance regulations for the banking industry as well as regulations restricting bank participation in domestic bond issues were maintained through the 1980s (though bank subsidiaries have recently been granted partial access to the securities industry), thus keeping the fences around the banking and securities businesses in place. The globalization of financial markets, however, has diminished the coherence and consistency of the regulatory framework, effective as it was in the high growth period. These changes could not but impact the effectiveness and capability of the main bank to carry out integrated ex ante, interim, and ex post monitoring.

Many leading industries had reached the international technological and marketing frontier by the 1990s. Ex ante credit assessments of projects on an uncertain technological and market trajectory require sophisticated skills in finance, engineering, and market analysis. The longstanding custom of relying on collateral in lieu of a credit assessment and domestic regulations prohibiting banks from engaging in securities underwriting have deterred banks from developing the sophisticated ex ante monitoring skills honed by investment banks and venture capital firms under the Anglo-American securities-based financial system.

The pitfalls of collateralism were shown most dramatically in the "Bubble" of the late 1980s and its aftermath. Banks competed fiercely to lend without proper project analysis as long as the loans were collateralized. As Stiglitz and Weiss argued, however, a collateral requirement alone, without proper ex ante monitoring of borrowers and their projects, may have an adverse selection effect.[4] Wealthier borrowers who were able to offer larger collateral may have been willing to take greater risks, while others may have simply been gamblers in land speculation. The banking sector turned into a cash-generating machine and the collective speculation mania continued until the Bubble burst in 1990–2.

The partial deregulation of bond issues may also have had detrimental effects on the interim monitoring capabilities of main banks. When a firm becomes less reliant on bank loans and is freed from the bank's implicit and explicit intervention, the incompetence or shirking of managers may not necessarily be bad news for main banks because such developments may increase the probability of a firms' return to bank loans. Thus, the main bank might have become lukewarm in performing interim monitoring. Also, the diversification by firms of settlement accounts among multiple banks, and the development of the securitization of loans, diminished the flow of information from firms to main banks, and consequently diminished the bank's ability to perform interim monitoring.

Deregulation had a subtle impact on the main bank's ex post monitoring. The declining rent opportunity for the main bank might have weakened its incentive to commit itself to costly rescue operations. The prospect of less intervention by the bank may have had positive incentive effects on workers and managers when the bank's bargaining power was strong (Chapter 4). However, when the bank's power to control had already been weakened below a certain threshold, a further decline in its bargaining power triggered a negative incentive effect on the insiders of the firm, as they became free from any external discipline.

The emergence of market financing and the development of the market for corporate control as a means of ex post monitoring are not the same thing, and a monitoring mechanism alternative to the main bank system for ex post monitoring has not yet appeared. Sales of holding stock by banks remain limited, and the managers of large firms are still insulated from the threat of takeovers. The legal prohibition on holding companies and the institutionalization of the internal board of directors combine to make the management of firms virtually free from external discipline, except for the discipline of the product market.

But does this mean the end of contingent governance? Is an alternative corporate governance structure feasible? Will path-dependent reforms to the main bank system continue to generate evolutionary responses to the

[4] Stiglitz and Weiss, pp. 393–410.

environmental changes taking place in the Japanese system? These future-oriented problems will be dealt with in the final chapter. Before broaching them, however, I will use the next section to present an outline of the developmental stage characteristics of the main bank system. I will then discuss their relevance to transition economies in the next chapter.

IMPLICATIONS FOR DEVELOPING ECONOMIES

As mentioned earlier, the regulatory framework of the Japanese main bank system maintained a low but positive real deposit. If the real deposit rate were to fall below zero because of high inflation, wealth would begin to shift from households to the government. If the government were to be able to indiscriminately distribute the wealth gained, nonproductive activities, or "rent-seeking" behavior, aimed at acquiring those gains would ensue and developing economies would stagnate. This was actually a widespread reality in Africa and Latin America in the 1970s. A situation in which the real deposit rate is negative because of inflation is generally called "financial repression." Murdoch, Hellmann, and Stiglitz differentiated between this situation and "financial restraint," in which the real deposit rate is low but is maintained at positive levels.[5] Since such a situation can be found not only in Japan, but also in the East Asian economies experiencing high growth, the implications for developing economies have recently become the focus of much attention.

Financial restraint has two effects on growth. First, if the savings interest rate elasticity is not high, it will not decrease the gross savings amount, but will produce rents in the banking sector. If bank management is adequately monitored, these rents will not be spent on nonproductive consumption, but will facilitate banks' expansions, such as branch openings, and will contribute to increased deposit formation.

On the other hand, if lending rates are also kept at levels lower than where they can on average clear the market, rents produced in the banking sector will spill over into the hands of the borrowing corporate sector. If, as discussed earlier, banks differentiate their lending rates through such practices as requiring the firm to hold compensating balances, rents will not be shared equally within the corporate sector. If loan interest rate decisions are made systematically rather than arbitrarily, this would have a certain incentive effect on the firm's activities. If loan interest rate decisions are determined based on the firm's growth potential or current

---

[5] Hellmann, Murdock, and Stiglitz, "Financial Restraint."

market share, this could theoretically be expected to stimulate productive "rent-seeking" behavior by the firm, motivating it to try to expand its market share. If, however, loan interest rate decisions are made on the basis of the historical relationship between the firm and the bank, this will contribute to the generation and maintenance of a main bank system, but is not at all likely to have a developmental effect.

Determining which effect has actually won out in Japan will require empirical analyses. Provisional calculations that I made on the basis of the financial report data of listed companies show that from the mid 1960s to the mid 1970s the lowest real borrowing rates were in the regulated electrical power industry, followed by the shipbuilding industry, a target of government industrial policies. By contrast, real borrowing rates in the automobile and electrical machinery industries, which were growth industries in this period, were higher overall than those of the textile industry. This somewhat unexpected result can be explained by the effect of history, or the longstanding relationship between banks and firms in the textile industry. However, the determination of whether or not the diffusion of bank rents throughout the industrial sector has a growth effect can only be made through serious empirical microanalysis.

Let us leave the solutions to these issues to future research, and turn now to outlining the three main developmental/historical situations in which the main bank system effectively spurred the economy on to high growth.

1. The basic technological and marketing knowhow useful for investing in the industries that played leading roles in the early high growth period had, with a few exceptions, already been developed abroad. The coordination of major complementary investments was conducted in the public domain through such forums as the Industrial Structure Council. The focus of ex ante monitoring by the private banking sector was, therefore, on the managerial and organizational capabilities of firms to absorb and refine existing knowledge. In this regard, the integration of ex ante and interim monitoring in the main bank was advantageous because continual interim monitoring provided city banks with the organization-specific knowledge not available to other financial institutions such as securities firms and trust banks.

2. In spite of Japan's considerable experience with private enterprise, international isolation and government control during the wartime period hindered the development of the specialized financial monitoring resources needed in a market oriented financial system. Thus, rather than dividing the financial monitoring function between investment banks,

commercial banks, credit rating companies, investment funds, and reorganization specialists, it was more practical to delegate monitoring to the banking sector in an integrated manner.

3. Immediately after the war, the capital bases of many firms were weakened by the cancellation of government wartime obligations. With limited residual output capabilities, stock issuance was not an effective means of raising investment capital. Given the weak financial capabilities of firms and their low profitability, the existence of banks that would commit to rescuing firms provided a suitable corporate governance structure. The Bank of Japan's postwar provision of capital to banks through the rediscounting of bills contributed to the formation of this corporate governance structure without shaking the managerial foundations of the banks.

Although these situations are all unique to postwar Japan, they may suggest some generic concepts that can be used in approaching the issue of corporate governance in today's transition economies.

6

Relevance to Corporate Governance in Transition Economies

COMPARATIVE INSTITUTIONAL ANALYSIS OF TRANSITION ECONOMIES

The study of transition economies, or economies in transition from communist planning to a market system, is a major focus of comparative institutional analysis. From the late 1980s to the early 1990s, when the communist political system in the Soviet Union and Central Europe suddenly began to collapse, optimism regarding the transition to market economics swelled. A clear-cut transition program had not been developed by the reform economists in these countries, and in its place was the simplistic libertarian belief that if political freedom were assured, the economic incentives of people who had long been suppressed would be released, naturally resulting in a free-market system. Staff members of the IMF and the World Bank as well as academic consultants from Harvard and MIT in the USA advised those economies to implement drastic price liberalization, to balance their fiscal budgets, and to privatize firms as quickly as possible. They especially emphasized the need for introducing a securities market and developing market monitoring institutions, such as investment funds, in order to cultivate capitalistic firms.

Unfortunately, such neoclassical prescriptions have not worked well in transition economies. As will be seen in the next section, the privatization of firms contributed less to the development of a market for corporate control than to the widespread emergence of insider control, whereby managers who had already carved out substantial controlling power by the end of the communist regime gained de jure control of their firms as well. These managers then enlisted other employees as their allies and attempted to construct their own empires free from external monitoring. In Russia, managers would at times entrust the Mafia with resolving emergent contractual disputes without regard for the market or legal discipline. Neoclassical prescriptions were extremely naive to the historical and evolutionary constraints entailed in the transition from a communist system.

In China, by contrast, the communist political system has been maintained as in the past and extreme caution is being taken in establishing an enterprise privatization program. An irreversible course toward the gradual corporatization of state-owned enterprises (SOEs) has already been chosen, but a conclusion has yet to be reached on who will be responsible for monitoring those firms. Will monitoring be conducted by a state-owned holding company or a decentralized banking system? Or does the development of a more liberal securities market need to be permitted? Such questions have only begun to be raised. Various forms of ownership have emerged through the growth of publicly owned enterprises at the local township and village level, the spinning off of corporate subsidiaries by SOEs, and the experimental public listing of stocks by elite SOEs. It is on the basis of these forms of ownership that economic development is proceeding at a rapid pace.

This situation suggests that a comparative institutional perspective is needed to consider the institutional problems involved in the transition from planned to market-based economics. For example, why is China displaying better economic performance than Russia and Central Europe? Is it because the former entered the transition from a later stage of development still characterized by a heavy reliance on agriculture? Does it point to the generic supremacy of the gradual approach as opposed to the Big Bang approach in transition? If attempts to imitate the Anglo-American system using the Big Bang approach are constrained by historical and evolutionary circumstances, what type of market economy can serve as a model for transition economies? Does such a model even exist?

A major purpose of this book has been to apply the methods of comparative institutional analysis to the Japanese economy. Though I am not a specialist in the field of transition economics, this chapter attempts to examine the relevance of this analytical framework to corporate governance, a major issue facing transition economies. It must be emphasized beforehand that this is not being done to suggest that the Japanese model will suffice as a model for transition economies. Nonetheless, it is important to recognize that some of the circumstances that helped shape the postwar Japanese system are very similar to the circumstances that can be seen in today's transition economies.

Chapter 1 suggested that insider control has emerged as a serious problem in today's transition economies. It was also already noted that the process of democratizing the wartime controlled economy in postwar

Japan held the same potential for insider control (Chapter 4). Stocks that were transferred to and consolidated in the Holding Company Liquidation Commission in the process of dismantling the *zaibatsu* are estimated to have accounted for 40 percent of the stocks outstanding in Japan at the time. The New Dealers in the GHQ who were in a position to exert a large influence in the process of settling these temporary devices of state ownership hoped to bring about "democratic" market control of enterprises through the diffusion of stockholding. That aspiration may have been similar to that of advisers in Russia and Poland in the early 1990s. The firm's employees were offered preferential stock purchasing rights, resulting in the outward appearance of decentralized stock ownership. Ultimately, however, this process resulted in the elimination of the remnants of classical capitalist control that had once existed in Japan, and in the emergence of autonomous managers who shared much of their gains with other workers. The response to the possible hazard of insider control evolved in the formation of successive financial *keiretsu* and the accompanying development of a contingent governance structure. Can the threat of insider control in Russia and Central Europe also be dealt with by creating some similar structure of contingent governance? In China, can some kind of institutional measures be taken in the corporatization of enterprises to prevent the threat of insider control from arising?

In addition to the various similarities that can be seen between Japan in the postwar period and today's transition economies, there are naturally some significant differences as well. Firms in wartime Japan were under strict bureaucratic control, and the so-called "reformist" bureaucrats that devised the control mechanisms gleaned some of their ideas from studying the planning apparatus of the Soviet Union.[1] During the war, banks were used as tools of financial control and it was easy for the managers of munitions firms to obtain loans. Nevertheless, when the controlled economy of the wartime period ended, there existed a stock of managers experienced in market transactions. After the government announced that wartime obligations were going to be canceled, firms and banks alike were well aware that they could not survive without restructuring their debts and credits and making private efforts to strengthen their capital bases. Unlike postwar Japan, however, which had only limited connections with the outside world due to the control of the occupation forces, today's transition economies exist in an environment of highly developed

---

[1] Tetsuji Okazaki, "The Japanese Firm under the Wartime Planned Economy," in Aoki and Dore (eds.), *The Japanese Firm*, pp. 350–78.

international financial markets and information and communications technologies. The possible institutional developments in the transition economies are sure to be influenced by these external environmental factors.

Regardless of differences in historical circumstances, the problem of insider control is a universal threat in economies where the market for corporate control is undeveloped. As Sergei Braguinski recently warned, the insider control problem in Russia should not be seen by Japan today as somebody else's problem.[2] As we saw in the last chapter, the decrease in the monitoring capabilities of banks has created a vacuum in the external discipline over Japanese firms, a development that may prove to have been a cause of the Bubble and its aftermath. If the insider control problem is shared by these economies, then they also share the need to solve this problem by institutionalizing some form of contingent governance structure. Naturally, the specific shape of this structure will depend on the unique historical circumstances of each economy, but comparing the relationship between the historical circumstances in each economy and the potential for institutional evolution may help us gain a theoretical understanding of the mechanisms for dealing with the threat of insider control. As stated at the beginning of this book, comparisons of different economies can substitute for the laboratory experimentation that the social sciences lack. By striving to filter out the various historical conditions of different economies and to extract common evolutionary characteristics, we can expect to discover embedded patterns of institutional design that cannot be seen when performing a superficial examination of a single economy.

EMERGENT INSIDER CONTROL

This section presents a simple explanation of how and why there is a general tendency toward insider control in transition economies.[3] The term "insider control" refers to the phenomenon whereby the substantial portion of enterprise control rights are either legally or de facto captured by the managers (sometimes in collusion with other workers) of former SOEs in the process of being privatized (corporatized) in former commu-

---

[2] *Nihon Keizai Shinbun*, Fall 1994.

[3] The remainder of this chapter draws on ch. 1 of Masahiko Aoki and Hyung-Ki Kim (eds.), *Corporate Governance in Transitional Economies: Insider Control and The Role of Banks*, Washington, DC: Economic Development Institute of the World Bank, 1995, pp. 3–29.

nist economies. Insider control in this sense is an evolutionary phenomenon that emerges as a legacy of communism. When the stagnation of
communist regimes deepened in the 1970s and 1980s in Central and
Eastern Europe, central planning bureaucrats tried to overcome the crisis
by relinquishing most of the planning instruments, such as investment
and pricing decisions, to the management of SOEs. In this process, the
managers built up an irreversible jurisdictional authority within their
own SOEs. The gradual retreat of the central planning authority ended
with its sudden dismantling. The managers of SOEs who had already
carved out substantial controlling rights from the planning apparatus
further enhanced their rights in the vacuum created by the collapse of the
communist state. There seems to be nobody who has obvious legal or
political power to dismiss the managers of ex-SOEs so long as they have
the support of their workers.

The other characteristic of the communist regime that constrained the
worker's freedom of job choice was their de facto job security. Workers
were provided with medicare, child care, leisure facilities, housing, pensions, and other services by the employing SOE. They had a large stake in
the employing enterprise. After the collapse of communism and the end
of its "egalitarian" ideology, the workers were threatened by the possibility
of losing those vested interests. The more uncertain became the outcome
of the corporatization of their enterprises, the greater was the threat to
their livelihoods. Their inevitable opposition to enterprise privatization
may have to be overcome by virtually giving them a substantial portion of
the firm's assets.

Needless to say, the realization of the potential for insider control varies
across economies. Among the possible factors that determine the extent
of insider control, the most important are the degree of management
autonomy and the workers' strength against communist control in the
final stages of the communist regime, as well as the political autonomy of
the privatization authority against the various interest groups in the
transition process.

Poland lies at one end of this continuum. The Law on State Enterprises,
enacted in 1981 even before the fall of the communist regime, gave
workers' councils, composed of fifteen members elected by the employees, a powerful position analogous to the board of directors in capitalist
corporations, including the right to appoint managers. Once communist
control began to disintegrate, workers quickly moved to capture control
of the assets of the enterprise before any enterprise privatization
plans were introduced. The most common form of state property

transformation worked as follows. Rather than corporatizing, the viable SOE was "liquidated" and a new company, in which the majority of the workers of the liquidated SOE became stockholders, leased or bought the former SOE's assets. Ideas based on the advice of influential American economists to have the state establish investment funds that would hold the substantial block of shares of the privatized firms and monitor managers never reached fruition.

Russia is a case of strong manager control. The State Committee on Property Administration (GKI) which was charged with mass privatization has been deemed the most politically successful reform authority in Russia through its generous accommodation of the interests of those managers who had established a solid base of control rights under the communist regime.

Simply put, the privatization process in Russia consisted of three stages. In the first stage, as mandated by a Yeltsin decree in July 1992, all SOEs were corporatized and their shares were held initially by the state (the Federal Property Foundation). In the second stage, the workers chose from among three privatization benefit plans formulated by the GKI. In the final stage, a portion of the remaining shares were auctioned for vouchers that had been given to every Russian citizen, while the remainder were either sold in a package to investment tenders or kept by the Federal Property Foundation (or other state institution) for the next several years.

The full implications of the scheme are not yet entirely clear, but so far the insiders have overwhelmingly selected an option that would guarantee them a majority share. This option allows managers and workers to individually purchase a combined total of 51 percent of the equity at a low purchase price (at 1.7 times the July 1992 book value of assets), and allows employee pension funds to collectively hold an additional 5 percent. The managers can also increase their shares by purchasing vouchers in the market or by buying back shares from their own workers (who are given incentives to sell their shares tax-free). At the same time, investment funds that participate in voucher auctioning were initially limited to owning only 10 percent (raised to 25 percent after January 1994) of a single privatized SOE. The board of directors of the newly privatized SOE, before the first meeting of shareholders, is composed exclusively of insiders, except for representatives of the local GKI and the Property Foundation.

At the other end of the spectrum is the former German Democratic Republic (East Germany), whose privatization process was managed by the centralized privatization authority Treuhandanstaldt (THA). Even in

East Germany, however, asset stripping by the insiders was an imminent danger when the communist regime fell. The only factor that prevented the subsequent development of insider control was the centralized authority given to the THA and the institutional commitment to complete privatization by the end of 1994. The privatization of SOEs was completed predominantly through the partial or complete acquisition of assets by West German (former Federal Republic of Germany) corporations. In that sense, privatization in East Germany resembled a takeover in capital markets even though it was mediated by a centralized privatization agency. Even in this case, however, the end result of the transition was a corporate governance structure unlike the neoclassical model of stockholder sovereignty. In West German firms, law requires that insiders (worker representatives) occupy the same number of seats as stockholder representatives on the supervisory councils (board of directors) that appoints managers.

The Czech Republic and Hungary provide intermediate cases. The insiders were weaker under communism in these countries than in Poland or Russia, and the political power of the state (the privatization agency) in the transition process was weaker than in East Germany. As a result, the tendency toward insider control has not been completely resolved. Privatization in the Czech Republic is widely regarded as an ideal example of outside stockholder control realized through the distribution of "vouchers" that can be exchanged for shares of privatized firms. The reality is not so simple, however. The privatization process starts with competitive "privatization project" plans (which can be submitted by anyone) for a former SOE designated by the Ministry of Privatization, which has the sole authority to select a project. The Ministry has a political preference for projects that include the auctioning of shares for vouchers, but according to its own data, only 53 percent of the total book value of privatized enterprises have been exchanged for vouchers. The first preference of managers who were able to submit the most informative plans is said to have been for buying out the company themselves. The tendency toward insider control thus exists, but has been moderated by the centralization of project selection.

In Hungary, a system similar to the Polish structure of workers' councils was introduced in 1984 (Law on Enterprise Councils), though the relative authority of workers to managers was weak. The free-market oriented post communist government granted the enterprise councils the initiative to privatize, but, unlike the Czech approach, this scheme seems to have provided managers more room to maneuver in fending off outsider intervention. The majority of shares of privatized SOEs, with the exception of those purchased by overseas firms, are cross-owned by other firms, banks, and the state privatization authority, which has the right of final approval over privatization plans. Unfortunately, the unavailability of data makes it impossible to know the precise extent of cross-shareholding.

Thus, although there is a variation in degree, the tendency toward insider control is manifested in all of the former communist states of Eastern and Central Europe except in newly emergent entrepreneurial enterprises and joint ventures with foreign corporations. This is an evolutionary outcome of the legacies of the communist regime, which can be moderated only by a strong privatization agency.

This lesson may be especially instructive for China, which has now begun experimenting with various corporate governance structures. A corporate law was enacted in China at the end of 1993, but the pace at which the nearly 100,000 state-owned enterprises will be corporatized has not yet been determined. By 1993 there were already 3,800 joint stock companies and joint ventures, but the conversion of SOEs into joint stock companies has been limited to some of the stronger firms. It seems that even in these firms the Communist Party continues to exert influence on the selection of managers. Still, the signs of insider control are already unmistakable. In SOEs, worker demands for vested interests regardless of productivity increases are frequently criticized, even in government documents, as "the iron rice bowl." If SOEs are privatized without an effective external monitoring mechanism and these vested interests are legally ratified, insider control will have an enormous impact on the national economy.

One example of insider control emerging in China today is a scheme whereby managers of SOEs conspire with government authorities to convert the profitable divisions of their company into subsidiaries and then transfer favorable assets and productive workers to those subsidiaries. If a subsidiary actually makes a profit, it will become increasingly independent of the state. If it shows a loss, on the other hand, the state-owned parent company, and thus the state, has no choice but to rescue the firm since the state's corporatization program has not yet been fully implemented. In either case, the insiders are protected against the risks of privatization yet are still able to claim most of its possible gains.

Many such "non-state-owned enterprises," formed by insiders together with smaller township and village enterprises, are the driving force behind vital entrepreneurial initiative in China today, but they have been established at the cost of leaving nonvaluable assets and unproductive employees at the state-owned parent companies. The bad debt problems and "iron rice bowl" legacy of the remaining SOEs are some of the reasons that the government has hesitated to set deadlines and engage in full-fledged corporatization. However, the acquisition of state assets by some insiders may foster hostility from outsiders excluded from receiving those privileges. It may also weaken the ability and incentives of state-owned parent companies to restructure bad debts through their own efforts. To avoid this vicious cycle, discussion needs to focus on the government's commitment to a clear program of time limits and methods of SOE corporatization. But how can former SOEs that carry on the communist legacy of the "iron rice bowl" be monitored if they are corporatized? If they fail to consider this problem in advance, corporatization programs will be unable to efficiently reach their goals.

INADEQUACY OF INVESTMENT FUND MONITORING CAPABILITIES IN THE TRANSITION

Many economists have argued that the creation of investment funds (IFs) that hold a substantial block of shares of a privatized enterprise may serve as an effective external check on former SOEs. The hope of neoclassical economics is that the IFs would be interested in deriving dividends or capital gains made possible by efficiency-enhancing restructuring, while at the same time exerting sufficient pressure on the firm's management to implement that restructuring.

However, plans that seem similar to, but are actually different from, the IF scheme appear to be garnering a great deal of support from academics and policy makers in China today. According to these plans, even when an SOE is corporatized, a substantial portion of the shares is held by the state as in the past. State-owned holding companies then exercise the shareholder's rights. However, since it is impossible for a single holding company to exert control on upward of 100,000 firms, a layered structure of holding companies for the holding companies becomes necessary. The role of the stock market in such a system is not altogether clear, but it might be expected to play a significant and complementary role by forming stock prices.

In this section I first want to discuss the difficulties involved in trying to apply pure neoclassical ideas to economies in which insider control has either emerged or is threatening to emerge. Following that, I will present a criticism of the Chinese concept of layered holding companies.

First, a block of shares held by the IFs may not be sufficient to effectively control the privatized SOE if there is a substantial insider holding of shares (as was the case in Russia). How would the minority IFs be able to resist the majority power of the insiders in a critical situation requiring corporate restructuring through the dismissal of managers and massive labor shearing?

Second, IFs in Russia and Central Europe were formed as privatization intermediaries that were funded by vouchers either deposited by investors or purchased by the IF itself on the market. They are therefore under constant pressure to realize reasonable dividends for investors. If the securities market develops, however, paradoxically they may not be interested in monitoring individual enterprises. This is because, as already mentioned in Chapter 4, the IFs would be able to perform at least as well as the market by investing in the market index. To respond to this concern, it has been proposed in Poland and other former communist nations that the range of portfolio selection of the IFs be restricted. However, such a move would be inconsistent with the IF function of maximizing expected profits, and would effectively transform the IF into a holding company with a limited range of activity. But is an IF capable of performing as a holding company? The next point addresses this question.

Third, the privatized SOE may be in desperate need of additional funding for restructuring, but the IF, as a share-redistributing intermediary, may not be able to readily mobilize financial resources to meet such needs. Even if new financial resources could somehow be mobilized, the majority insider control would imply tremendous agency costs for equity financing. The management and workers may be interested in consuming potential residual on the job or using it to make additional wage payments before distributing it as dividends. The IF may be able to mediate bank loans for firms if it is controlled by a holding company that also controls a bank (as in Russia), or is owned by a bank (as in the Czech Republic). In either of these cases, however, a conflict of interests would arise. For example, the assets of the IF may have been heavily invested in a failing enterprise and the holding company may be willing to risk the depositors' assets to salvage it.

These points are not intended to deny any role for the IF or holding companies in the governance structure during the transition process. On the contrary, it may even be an indispensable institutional component in counteracting the ill effects of insider control. The point, however, is to argue that the IF alone may not be capable of halting the evolutionary tendency toward insider control in the transition process. Attempting to rely solely on the IF may actually prolong the transition process by encouraging insiders to try to reduce external discipline. Further, public policies that may be needed to foster the development of other potentially effective external monitoring institutions, such as banks, may lag behind.

Finally, let us consider the concept of layered holding companies in China. If an efficient securities market does not develop (it may not develop if the majority of shares are held by the government), how would the parent holding company assess the performance of its subsidiary holding companies? If there is no objective standard of financial gains, the parent holding company's assessment would become arbitrary. Also, the subsidiary holding company would have the informational advantage since it has access to on-site information of the firm. As has already been suggested, the motive force behind economic development in China today is its village and township enterprises. These are publicly owned firms controlled at the lowest level of local government by villages and townships, and the village and township governments are functioning well indeed as holding companies. These local governments are themselves subjected to effective monitoring though a mechanism that forces fierce competition among them for increased income and the capture of regional markets. In view of this situation, even if the public holding of shares of corporatized firms is necessary, the exercise of shareholder's rights can and should be decentralized at the lowest levels of government possible. The idea of a layered hierarchy of holding companies is a mere caricature of the neoclassical paradigm, and offers nothing more than a reproduction of the planning bureaucratic apparatus of the past.

SOFT BUDGETING BY FORMER STATE BANKS

The discussion thus far has probably led readers to expect what follows here. That is, some form of contingent governance, especially by banks, might be an effective way (even more effective than a securities market) to deal with the particular incentive problems of insider control. Even if former SOEs are corporatized and a majority of their shares are owned by either insiders or state asset management funds, the imminent threat of defaulting on a debt contract can trigger the transfer of corporate control rights to the firm's creditors. Unlike a stock contract, a debt contract can impose a penalty on poorly performing shareholders and managers by transferring control rights, regardless of the desires of the current stockholders. In this sense, a debt contract has the potential to serve as an effective monitoring tool in transition economies where the structure of ownership rights of corporatized SOEs is still fluid.

However, two issues must be closely examined to determine whether or not the potential benefits of such a debt contract can actually be administered by banks in transition economies. First is the inherited momentum toward "soft budgeting" (relaxation of budget constraints) that is characteristic of communist economic systems. The Hungarian economist Yanos Kornai has warned against the negative effects of soft budgeting since the 1970s, regarding it as the largest underlying problem sustaining the inefficiencies of communist planned economies.[4] Once state-owned firms under the communist system fell into financial distress, a state-owned bank, as a part of the planning apparatus, would provide additional financing and bail out the firm. Because, as noted above, there was no competitive labor market and the workers' livelihoods were thus dependent upon the survival of the employing firm, not even the autocratic communist state had the political expedience to defend itself against the potential for mass unemployment. That is, the tendency toward soft budgeting and insider control were two sides of the same coin under the communist system. Also, even if an investment project should not have been ex ante implemented, it may become ex post efficient to make that firm survive once the initial investment was sunk in the firm.[5] If the firm could anticipate being rescued by the bank during times of financial distress, the insiders would lose their incentive to increase efficiency. The theoretical reason why the contingent governance structure designed in Chapter 4 contained a liquidation region below the rescue region that imposes strict penalties on insiders was precisely to control the adverse incentive effects caused by ex post soft budgeting.

The tendency toward soft budgeting by state banks under communism is highly likely to be inherited by commercial banks in transition economies in a path dependent manner. This is because banks that engage in corporate lending are the direct descendants of formerly state-owned banks, and many firms are former SOEs that had racked up bad debt under communism and during the transition phase. The safety net of social services provided by the state in market economies, such as social security and health insurance, has not been fully developed in the transition period. The burden of this deficiency is being borne by firms in the

---

[4] Janos Kornai, *The Socialist System: Political Economy of Communism*, Oxford and New York: Oxford University Press, 1992.

[5] Mathias Dewatripont and Eric Maskin, "Credit and Efficiency in Centralized and Decentralized Economies," *Review of Economic Studies*, Vol. 62 (1995), pp. 541–55.

form of excess employment. Corporate managers would not hesitate to justify the need for additional bank financing through collusion with politicians and bureaucrats under the old system. As we will see later, "policy financing" conducted by formerly state-owned specialized banks, which accounts for the majority of bank financing in Russia today, is not conducted as a part of an overall planned industrial policy, but is a disguised form of state subsidization and thus a legacy of communist era soft budgeting.

In addition to ex post soft budgeting that accommodates poor management after the fact, there are also incentives for both firms and banks toward what must be called ex ante soft budgeting. One of the problems for firms and banks in China (and other transition economies) today is that owing to a situation of financial repression in which the inflation rate exceeds the regulated lending interest rate, firms expect to accrue rents by maximizing their debts. In spite of the situation of financial repression, however, bank deposits by the household sector have increased, reaching a level of 46 percent of GDP in 1991. Former specialized banks (the Agricultural Bank of China, Industrial and Commercial Bank of China, Bank of Communications, People's Construction Bank of China, etc.) that have been converted into commercial banks have a strong incentive to lend to firms with high growth potential as long as they have collateral. Also, collusion has occurred between the managers of enterprises vying for loans and the lending managers of commercial banks, resulting in inefficient resource distribution inclined toward real estate investments. The problem, as has already been pointed out however, is that, even for investment projects that should not have been adopted ex ante, it became profitable (or less unprofitable) for the bank to continue that lending once the initial investment was sunk. The lack of incentives for lenders to conduct ex ante monitoring is creating the likelihood that additional financing will have to be provided later. To avoid the threat of soft budgeting, it is absolutely essential to have in place healthy macroeconomic policies that maintain real interest rates at positive levels.

The second problem facing transition economies with regard to soft budgeting is whether or not an approximate realization of a theoretically constructed ideal banking system capable of overcoming the insider control and soft budgeting problems would be possible in light of the various historical and evolutionary conditions of each transition economy. In Russia over the past several years, for example, more than a thousand new banks have cropped up alongside the spinoffs of former state-owned specialized banks. In China, by contrast, aside from the countless credit union type of financial institutions at the village and township level, several former state-owned specialized banks have been converted into commercial banks, and private banks have been established as joint ventures with capital from Hong Kong in a handful of provinces. The People's Bank of China (the central bank), which is said to employ more than 170,000 people, is believed to be exerting its political influence on the distribution of loans as it did in the past. These two economies are at opposite ends of the spectrum in terms of their banking structures during the transition, but will they be able to evolve into healthy banking systems that can perform ex ante, interim, and ex post monitoring? Are some kind of public policies and structural reform needed for banks to end the tendency toward soft budgeting and to engage in orderly ex ante and ex post monitoring practices? Is it possible for banks to restructure their past bad debts to firms without disrupting the normal production activities of those firms in order to break the vicious cycle of soft budgeting?

In the last chapter I said that one of the merits to be elicited from an historical overview of the Japanese main bank system is its ability to deal with a scarcity of monitoring resources by integrating the three stages of monitoring. However, the international environment in which transition economies exist today is wholly different from the environment of international isolation that Japan experienced in the postwar period. There is a plentiful international supply of resources for monitoring the operations of a securities-based system, including account audits, corporate asset assessments, investment project creditworthiness assessments, and fund management in the market. In Russia, strong investment funds are often managed either in conjunction with foreign securities firms or on the basis of consultations with such firms. Even in China, the special skills required for the auditing and securitization of joint ventures and subsidiaries of former SOEs are supplied by Hong Kong.

Considering the institutional inertia keeping the former state-owned banks from developing the monitoring capabilities needed in a market economy, a program for restraining the development of the securities market and promoting the development of the banking system as it existed in postwar Japan is neither desirable nor feasible. It has already been pointed out, however, that the tendency toward insider control and the lack of a defined privatization program for ex-SOEs also makes it difficult to wholly entrust the securities markets in transition economies with the exclusive functions of corporate financing and monitoring. Thus, a two-fronted approach is one option for transition economies. That is, rather than pursuing ways to provide an external check on enterprises by trying to develop either the securities market or the banking system, it is better in the transition period to strive to develop those systems simultaneously. The spontaneous evolution of those institutions through competition will determine which will become prevalent in the post-transition period.

The evolutionary approach to the selection of financial systems in transition economies is preferable in the presence of complementarity with other systemic elements, an already much-emphasized concept. Recall that a mode of governance in which the bank and the insiders share control rights (as in Germany), or in which control rights shift between the bank and the insiders contingent upon the financial state of the firm (as in Japan), would be complementary to firms committed to the continuous employment of workers and to internal training. The market-oriented approach to corporate control, by contrast, is complementary to the market-oriented approach to the formation and utilization of specialized skills. How are the patterns of labor organization and skill formation in firms in transition economies likely to evolve in the future?

One scenario may be that the hierarchical aspect of the work organization in the SOE would be reformed such that task assignments in the organization are made more on the basis of individuated functional skills. In this scenario, the complementary development of the capital market institutions would be necessary because the internal efficiency of such an organization can best be measured by the residual after competitive payments for individual skills. An alternative scenario may be that the collegial aspects of work organization in former SOEs develop into a team-oriented work organization based on assimilated knowledge. In this scenario, the development of banking institutions would be complementary. Still other scenarios may be feasible. The transition economy may take advantage of its latecomer status by developing a hybrid of the two organizational modes, selecting a mode suitable for the nature of each particular industry. Or, if the transition economy fails to develop appropriate corporate governance and financial institutions, it might fall into long-term stagnation. No one can be sure which of these scenarios will or should be chosen. We may posit, however, that an eclectic approach in which the securities market and banking institutions are developed simultaneously is an option in the transition process.

HOW TO CONTROL INSIDER CONTROL?

This section discusses a theoretical mechanism for restraining the tendency toward soft budgeting by banks and for providing external discipline on insider control. It also considers the question of whether this mechanism is complementary to the existence of securities markets and investment funds. The final section presents a brief commentary on banking institution reform in transition economies that approximate the proposed mechanism.

Assume that all of the former SOEs under communism are corporatized. Although these would be held under various forms of ownership, let us assume that they become public companies the majority of whose shares are held either by asset management funds of the state, or individually or collectively by company insiders. Let us also assume that the company is wholly controlled by the managers, and that the appointment and dismissal of these managers is beyond the direct control of outside investors. In spite of such incomplete privatization, there are still several advantages to corporatizing ex-SOEs that were previously mere administrative units in the state's planning apparatus.

First, managers are responsible for preparing financial reports, such as balance sheets and profit and loss statements, and are subject to external monitoring in the form of audits. This helps make the management of the firm more transparent. Second, the board of directors legally holds, at the very least, the right to appoint and dismiss managers. This leaves little room for the arbitrary appointment and dismissal of managers for political reasons even if a large number or a majority of shares is held by the state. As a result, insider control by the managers may grow stronger, but once the firm is corporatized, there can be a mechanism for correcting it in critical situations.

Suppose that these insider-controlled enterprises are somehow freed of the burden of their past bad debts through loan rescheduling or cancellation, but that their survival and growth require an injection of outside investment capital. In this case, the one bank that has a close relationship with the firm and manages its major settlement accounts will become a lead bank (LB) and will organize a loan syndicate with many other banks. The LB may own a minority share, possibly converted from past loans, of the borrowing enterprise up to a certain limit (say 5 percent). By combining its position as a minority shareholder with its role of performing the commercial banking function, the LB will have an information advantage over other lending institutions regarding the borrowing firm. The question is how this advantage can be utilized to reduce agency costs of external financing as well as monitoring costs, rather than being used by the LB to exploit its private benefits at the cost of other banks and investors.

Suppose the LB is limited to providing only a minority share, say 20 percent, of the syndicate loans, but that the LB must guarantee the repayment of a certain percentage of the claims of other member banks. This imposes a heavy responsibility on the LB. In return, however, the LB may charge a syndicate management premium while enjoying the benefits of running the payment settlement and deposit accounts of the borrowing enterprise.

If the enterprise becomes unable to meet repayment obligations, the LB is obliged to buy the defaulted claims, up to the agreed upon limit, of syndicate member banks. The LB then converts these debts into new equity. The LB either auctions off the new shares to reorganization specialists or other firms, or holds them for a specified period of time (two years, for example). In the latter case, the LB exercises its newly obtained shareholder rights to restructure the defaulting enterprise by replacing the managers, laying off workers, liquidating assets, etc. If the insiders refuse to cooperate, the LB may threaten to invoke liquidation procedures, but a safety net of social services, including unemployment insurance and pensions, is provided by the state when a firm is corporatized. After restructuring within the said period, the LB may sell the amount of shares beyond the normal limit (5 percent, for example) for possible capital gains. In either case, the defaulting insider-controlled enterprise would be transformed into an outsider-controlled enterprise through a debt–equity swap, while the insiders would be penalized for debt default by the loss of their share values, and possibly the loss of their employment continuation values as well. If there is no prospect for capital gains from restructuring, the LB may decide to liquidate the defaulting enterprise. In this case the unrecovered value of debts would be borne by the LB.

This institutional framework resembles the plan for modifying bankruptcy procedures proposed by Philippe Aghion, Oliver Hart, and John Moore.[6] In their model, however, bankruptcy procedures are administered by the court, while in our model they are the responsibility of the LB because of its clear information advantage for making the decision of whether to restructure or liquidate. Also, since the LB itself has to bear the

---

[6] Philippe Aghion, Oliver Hart, and John Moore, "The Economics of Bankruptcy Reform," *Journal of Law, Economics and Organization*, Vol. 8 (1992), pp. 523–46.

costs of bankruptcy by partially guaranteeing the debts of other institutions, it would be motivated to conduct earnest ex ante and interim monitoring when forming the syndicate.

Generally speaking, from the point of view of the bank, there are trade-offs between the diversification of lending risk and incentives to monitor. An arm's-length relationship between the bank and the borrower will allow the bank to diversify risk, but will weaken incentives to monitor. An exclusive lending relationship, however, not only will expose the bank to idiosyncratic risk, but also may dilute its commitment to ex post monitoring because once a loan is made, the bank may be tempted to engage in soft budgeting to rescue the firm. As noted above, the bank tries to balance risk diversification and incentives to perform ex ante and interim monitoring by partially guaranteeing the debts of other institutions. Further, since control rights automatically shift to outsiders through a debt–equity swap when an enterprise defaults, the failed managers cannot evade penalties. The LB, or the restructuring agent (purchasing firm) that buys the shares from the LB, thus has incentives to restructure for capital gains. As opposed to the ordinary reorganization by creditors, the LB or restructuring agent can secure future returns to restructuring costs without fearing the emancipation of the rescued enterprise. Thus, premature liquidation may be avoided, while the threat of punishing poorly performing insiders is made credible.

Finally, the above framework does not exclude the development of the securities market, but is complementary to it. Instead of forming a loan syndicate, for example, the LB could also underwrite the debt bond issuance of its client firms and guarantee their payment. Price assessments in the market would compete with the LB's interim monitoring and might counteract the errors or moral hazard problems of the LB. Also, if privatized investment funds can develop as restructuring specialists, they may also be able to submit bids to the LB for equity converted from debt.

BANKING REFORM

Although the case for the development of a sound banking system in the transition process appears to be strong, the current state of banking institutions in transition economies seems to be far from that needed to perform the kind of tasks suggested above. Is there any hope that they will develop the capacity and incentives to do so?

In the transition economies of Eastern and Central Europe, most of the banks, with the exception of a few foreign banks, are either successors or spinoffs of former state banks or newly established agent banks of corporatized SOEs. Large commercial banks in Central Europe were created over the last few years as a result of the split of the former state monobank into a central bank and a number of commercial banks. Loan portfolios were distributed to the new commercial banks along regional (Poland) or sectoral lines (Czech Republic, Hungary). Most of the deposits are with specialized savings institutions, and are being refinanced to commercial banks through central banks. The spinoffs of the former state banks are still owned by the state, which is either investigating their privatization (Poland, Hungary) or has already privatized their majority ownership (Czech Republic). Private commercial banks have been established recently, but the former state banks are still dominant in assets. In Russia there are now approximately two thousand independent commercial banks. About seven hundred of these, including most of the larger banks, are spinoffs of former Soviet specialized banks (savings banks, agricultural and construction banks, etc.), which are now primarily owned by former SOEs.

The problem with former state banks is the provision of soft credit unaccompanied by ex ante monitoring (ex ante soft budgeting). Half of all commercial bank loans extended in Russia in 1992 were for policy financing funded by the Central Bank or the national budget.[7] These banks, in other words, served to channel national funds to former SOEs.

The newly created agent banks have their own problems. In Russia more than a thousand agent banks have been created from scratch since 1990. Most of these were set up by enterprises or groups of enterprises to manage their cash flows and to perform payment settlements on their behalf. These banks also engage in lending and exchange speculation, but they are still behaving less like commercial banks than like spinoffs of the financial departments of firms. Because all SOEs under communism held accounts at state banks through which their transaction settlements were automatically handled, they did not internally develop the financial management skills needed in a market economy. However, it is widely known that the imperfection of the system for legally enforcing contracts in the transition period sometimes made it possible for banks to resort to the private enforcement of difficult transaction settlements. Since these

---

[7] World Bank, "The Banking System in Transition: Russia," Europe and Central Asia Department Report 12763, Washington, DC: World Bank, 1993.

banks cannot by nature function as independent monitoring agents for firms, they may be overexposed to the idiosyncratic risks of their client firms.

For banks to operate on a sound credit basis, their assets must be sufficiently diversified. When the capital basis of the bank is thin, however, as is the case with most agent banks, it is nearly impossible to diversify lending while meeting the capital requirements of the parent enterprises. The sheer number of agent banks and their small size makes it difficult to develop loan syndicates because of the difficulty in reaching agreements regarding which bank ought to bear responsibility for syndicate organization and how to establish the priority of claims.

In spite of these problems, however, the banking sector in transition economies appears to be gradually evolving as a viable institution. Peter Dittus, who has studied the banking systems in the Central European economies in great detail, has noticed a recent increase in the spread between bank deposit and lending rates, as well as a recent decline in their net lending to enterprises.[8] After careful examination, he suggests that the decline in lending is a result not of a credit crunch caused by a government deficit, but of a bank's hardening of budget constraints (budget hardening) toward enterprises. He cautiously notes: "clearly, the environment in which banks are operating and their behavior have changed much more than seems to be commonly acknowledged. It has also become evident, however, that the difficulties that remain to be overcome are substantial." Elena Belyanova, a scholar of note, and Ivan Rozinsky, a researcher and banker, indicates that the differences between the spinoffs of the former state banks and the newly created banks are beginning to blur, and that some of them seem to be evolving as viable banking institutions.[9] Among these, a small number of "export sector banks" are using foreign currencies to provide interim lending to export firms, and are using high salaries to attract talented personnel with monitoring skills. They claim that these banks are also performing continuous interim monitoring of borrowing firms.

What difficulties have to be overcome for the better banks to evolve into active monitors of insider control? Let us try to identify several of the basic problems to be addressed.

[8] Peter Dittus, "Corporate Governance in Central Europe: The Role of Banks," mimeo, Bank of International Settlements, Basle, 1994.

[9] Elena Belyanova and Ivan Rozinsky, "Evolution of Commercial Banking in Russia and the Implications for Corporate Governance," in Aoki and Kim (eds.), *Corporate Governance*, pp. 185–213.

The first is the dilemma between risk diversification and monitoring mentioned earlier. The bank should diversify its loans in order to avoid the softening of lending standards and the excessive exposure to idiosyncratic risks associated with relational lending. One way to do this, as noted earlier, is to form loan syndicates, but this may dilute the incentives of the bank to monitor.

The second problem involves the social costs of bankruptcy. The mechanical application of bankruptcy procedures would be unproductive given the current state of transition economies. Since a sound payment system has not yet developed, many firms are dependent on interbank credit. Consequently, default by one large enterprise could cause a chain reaction of debt default, pushing many potentially viable firms into bankruptcy. The public registration system for ownership rights (over land assets, etc.) also remains undeveloped, and bankruptcy procedures involve the costs of maintaining a system of commercial courts. Newly corporatized SOEs seem to need outside financing, and sometimes subsidies, to remain viable. How can such financing and subsidies be provided without perpetuating a soft credit relationship between the bank and the enterprise?

In Russia, these challenges seem to be beyond the reach of decentralized small banks. To emancipate banks from fragmented, exclusive relational banking, the minimum capital requirement for banks needs to be drastically increased. Such regulations would provide an impetus for acquisitions and mergers among banks. Further, limiting the lending of a bank to a single enterprise – to one-quarter of the bank's capital, for example – would compel banks to restrain their volume of exclusive lending. Nevertheless, the purpose here is not to promote Anglo-American-style "arm's-length banking" as advised by the World Bank. This would only perpetuate a monitoring vacuum in transition economies such as Russia where insider control has developed.

Because many banks are now owned by enterprises, a movement toward arm's-length banking following the Anglo-American system will not evolve in any case. Through the process of merger and acquisition, formerly close bank–enterprise relationships may be somewhat loosened, but will be maintained with some distance. The enterprise would be likely to hold major payment settlement accounts with only a few banks. Of further interest are the regulations governing bank shareholding. The Ministry of Finance that oversees bank administration in Russia advocates German-style universal banking in which there are no restrictions on shareholding by banks, while the GKI – the privatization agent said to be striving toward the development of an Anglo-American style securities market – wants to implement Glass–Steagal type regulations which prohibit commercial banks from owning stocks. The compromise that has resulted from the political battle between the two is a rule that limits banks to holding a maximum 10 percent of a firm's shares. This restriction may have laid a foundation for the Russian banking system to develop in a fashion similar to the Japanese main bank system. In any case, banks that develop historical relationships with firms via many channels, including settlement accounts, loans, shareholding, etc., would be likely candidates for the role of lead bank if the need for lending diversification should lead to organized syndication.

China, by contrast, needs more decentralization in its banking system. As stated earlier, though former specialized banks have been transformed into commercial banks, they still hold oligopolistic power and are a breeding ground for soft-budgeting-prone policy financing. Also, the People's Bank of China (the central bank) still employs as many as 170,000 people and is exercising decision-making authority regarding the interbank distribution of capital. To help the bank develop sound monitoring capabilities, a substantial portion of the People's Bank of China could be divided and spun off into commercial banks, for example, while entry into commercial banking activities could be liberalized. The People's Bank would then have to limit itself to supplying growth capital on the basis of sound commercial transactions, such as rediscounting commercial bills and export bills, and would have to clearly separate itself from the field of financing so that the necessary financial aid to firms could be supplied through fiscal revenues.

A major financial reform issue in China today is whether shareholding by commercial banks should be allowed. The mainstream view favors the Glass–Steagal regulatory model. However, since commercial banks are allowed to own investment banks as subsidiaries, it is questionable whether the original goal of protecting the depositors' risk from equity speculation risk can be met. If the banking system and securities market are to be expected to develop simultaneously, then authorities may need either to institutionalize the establishment of pure holding companies that can concurrently control both securities and banking operations as separate subsidiaries, or to create a barrier between banking and securities operations and allow banks to hold only as many shares as necessary for monitoring their client firms.

However, the question of what kind of financial system reforms are needed is closely related to how the corporate governance structure evolves, and is not, needless to say, a question that can be easily answered in isolation.

POSTSCRIPT: CHINA'S EXPERIMENT WITH THE MAIN BANK SYSTEM (1997)

In the summer of 1996, China's central bank issued the Temporary Rule for Main Bank Control and started experimenting with relational financing among three hundred large state-owned enterprises (SOEs) and four state-owned commercial banks in seven large cities, including Beijing and Shanghai.[10] One bank was assigned to each of those SOEs as its "main bank" (*zhuban yinhang*), with some overlapping, just as in the designated banking system in wartime Japan. Those banks were expected to provide loan contracts to their SOEs without government intervention, while jointly working out a possible solution to the latter's bad debt problems.

As noted, banks might be counted as possible candidates for external agents that could work jointly with SOEs to resolve bad debt problems, even though the monitoring and restructuring expertise of existing banks is admittedly extremely low. However, we are not living in the first-best world, and any solution to resolving the problems of the socialist legacy needs to be sought in that particular historical context. Practical experimentation, so characteristic of the Chinese, is at least worth a try in the realm of main bank relationships.

In this regard, the Japanese experience after the war is instructive. In the summer of 1946 the Japanese government repudiated its guarantee of bank credits, as well as government debts and insurance obligations, to munitions companies, in order to control rising inflation. (The size of the loss from the repudiation is estimated at almost 20 percent of GNE in 1946.) The financial institutions and specific companies hit by the government's actions were made to separate balance sheets into old and new accounts. Debts and capital were placed into old accounts, and entries into new accounts were limited to those assets deemed absolutely necessary for current operations (such as inventories, cash). The amounts of those assets were then recorded as accounts payable to the old account. "The idea behind the operation was to clean up bad loans (alternatively

---

[10] This postscript is drawn from a chapter co-authored with Serdar Dinç entitled "Relational Financing as an Institution and Its Viability under Competition," in Masahiko Aoki and Gary R. Saxonhouse (eds.), *Finance, Governance, and Competitiveness in Japan*, Oxford and New York: Oxford University Press, 2000.

debts) [in old accounts] without interfering with ongoing . . . business."[11]
The two accounts were to be merged after reorganization, as was indeed
done after several years of joint work between companies and their designated banks. Hoshi described this process in detail and pointed out that
the close relationships and information sharing that developed between
firms and banks (former designated banks) during this process were
indeed instrumental to the evolution of the later-day main bank relationship as an institution.

We cannot tell yet whether the current Chinese experiment on the joint
workout between SOEs and banks will contribute to a solution to the bad
debt problem.[12] However, we should not lightly dismiss the experiment,
either. Without doubt, the state-owned banks may not have sufficient
expertise and competence to resolve bad debt problems of their own and
their client SOEs. There may always be a temptation for the banks to
indulge in soft budgeting in the anticipation of help from the state.
However, the People's Bank of China seems to be currently committed to
harder budgeting. Also, learning-by-doing is an essential ingredient for
banks to nurture reorganizational expertise and accumulate specific
information regarding client firms which may eventually be able to afford
banks with information rents.

One concern I have, however, is the limited number of banks involved
in the experiment. As discussed theoretically in Chapter 4, for an institution of relational financing to emerge as a socially beneficial institution,
the number of competing banks should be neither too large nor too small.
In China now, only four state-owned commercial banks converted from
specialized policy banks are operating in each province, together with, at
most, a few business enterprise-owned or province-owned banks and a
newly organized commercial bank which is consolidating local credit
cooperatives (i.e. the City Bank in Beijing). Further, the Industrial and
Commercial Bank has an excessively large share of contracting in the
main bank experiment (with 277 SOEs out of the 300 experimental sub-
jects).[13] No bank may voluntarily want relational financing with SOEs
that are having greater problems without the assurance of monopoly
rents. However, too small a number of banks will restrain competition,
which may not be conducive to the development of a healthy relational

---

[11] Takeo Hoshi, "Cleaning up the Balance Sheet: Japanese Experience in the Postwar
Reconstruction Period," in Aoki and Kim (eds.), *Corporate Governance*, p. 307.
[12] There was an optimistic interim report on this experiment in the international edition
of *The People's Daily* on January 8, 1997.
[13] Ibid.

financing institution. What is absolutely necessary for the successful transition of the Chinese economy to a market economy is the further decentralization of the banking sector, which may be achieved by breaking up existing state-owned commercial banks, while allowing easier entry into the banking sector. Obviously, the introduction of more competition into the banking sector cannot be completely *laissez-faire* and needs to be framed within prudent regulation. In particular, the introduction of substantial capital reserve requirements should be placed on competing banks so that supervision over banks becomes rule-based and automatic.

Gains from Diversity and Institutional Reform in the Japanese Economy

COMPARATIVE ADVANTAGE IN JAPAN, THE US AND CHINA, AND THE STRUCTURE OF COMPLEMENTARITY

Whereas the last chapter dealt with transition problems in former planned economies, this chapter considers the transition potential of the institutional structure of the Japanese economy. Until now, this book has treated the Japanese economy as a system with mutual complementarity between its various institutions, and with a comparative advantage in the high engineering fields. It would be extremely difficult, however, to say that the economy has the potential to achieve absolute dominance in every industrial field, or that it is evolving into a system that will be able to fully maximize the gains from diversity. As can be deduced from the previous chapters, such an economic structure has yet to be found anywhere in the world.

Can the Japanese institutional structure evolve in such a way as to maintain and expand the industrial fields in which it holds the comparative advantage, given a changing international environment and the potential evolution of individual skill formation? Or is the inertia-driven Japanese institutional structure in danger of losing its long-held comparative advantage even in the high engineering fields, confronted as it is on both flanks by potential new industrial powers such as China on the one hand, and organizational reforms taking place in the USA on the other? Should Japan complete its transition to the "advanced" Anglo-American type of system as quickly as possible in order to avert this danger? Or should it rather attempt to make piecemeal changes to existing institutions so as to realize gains from diversity? Is the latter even feasible in view of complementarity between existing institutions?

I have argued in this book that one of the sources of Japan's comparative advantage in the field of high engineering is the nature of the internal information system of the firm. This is not necessarily in complete opposition to the classical approach, which explains comparative advantage in an industry by the relative supply of the basic factors of production – land, labor, and capital. However, the classical approach cannot fully explain intra-industry trade potential, like why Japanese firms have the comparative advantage in the development and production of memory chips while American firms have the comparative advantage in logic chips. The new trade theory of Elhanan Helpman and Paul Krugman accounted for these phenomena by factors of product differentiation and increasing returns, but their analysis does not fully explain the causes behind these factors themselves.[1] The firm continues, as before, to be treated as a black box. However, the potential for increasing returns is closely, though not exclusively, linked to learning by an organization, thus suggesting that it is also related to differences in the ability of organizations to function as information systems. In this book it is asserted that on-site information processing itself is the most important determinant of production efficiency, but that various organizational forms may evolve as a result of the inevitable bounded rationality of individuals and organizations. I also contend that the question of which organizational mode will become prevalent in a given economy depends largely on that society's history and institutional structure.

Let us once again summarize the features of the Japanese organizational mode from this perspective. First, each task unit operates on the basic organizational principles of information sharing and joint decision making, to which it adds individuated information processing as the information processing capabilities of individuals increase or information technologies develop. In Chapter 2 this organizational mode was referred to as a "horizontal hierarchy," in that information sharing is emphasized, while individuated information processing is only of secondary importance. For this mode to be used effectively, contextual skills must be formed and accumulated within the context of the organization, or through the process more commonly known as "on-the-job training." With the evolution of the horizontal hierarchy, contextual skills have evolved gradually into what Kazuo Koike calls "wide-ranging skills," useful not only in teamwork and communication, but also in individuated specialized functions.[2]

[1] Elhanan Helpman and Paul Krugman, *Market Structure and Foreign Trade*, Cambridge, MA: MIT Press, 1985.   [2] Koike, "Skill Formation Systems in the US and Japan."

In the Anglo-American system, by contrast, the prevalent mode until recently was the "functional hierarchy," in which information regarding the systemic environment was handled by the managers while only information regarding the separate idiosyncratic environments was left to be processed by the lower ranking workers. However, the development of digital communications technologies has had a remarkable effect on the processing and transmission of information in organizations with this information structure. Now the lower ranks of the hierarchy have easy access to information on the systemic environment extending beyond the boundaries of their idiosyncratic environments, and can use that information in their individual decision making. In organizations or social environments where the specialization of skill formation has evolved, however, these kinds of developments will prevent evolution toward an organizational mode based on information assimilation. Rather, they will result in the creation of organizations with a decentralized hierarchy in which each individual interprets a wide range of information and uses it in the decision-making process.

Both of these new developments require that each individual simultaneously processes information regarding the broad systemic environment and information regarding his or her specific idiosyncratic environment, and both are made possible by developments in the education system and information technologies. These organizations have a higher informational efficiency than primitive homogeneous teams or traditional functional hierarchies. (In terms of Figure 2 (in Chapter 2), this means that the middle region in both the top and bottom layers is expanding leftward as well as rightward.) If individual task units of Japanese organizations (assimilated information structures) were to gradually internalize and intensify their processing of information regarding idiosyncratic environments, and if those of American organizations were to expand their processing of information regarding the systemic environment, it might seem as though the Japanese and American organizational modes would converge. We must remember, however, that these two countries have followed very different historical paths. That is, in one case information on the systemic environment within the organization is processed jointly on an ad hoc basis, while in the other it is processed by individual task units according to formalized data sharing and certain organizational rules. This difference has long been thought to be a crucial determinant of comparative industrial advantage between the USA and Japan.

The evolution of organizations with a differentiated information structure in America is likely to increase those organizations' comparative advantage in any field where complementarity between tasks within the organization can be reduced. This does not mean that firms will sit back and wait for the technological developments that would make this possible. If controlling complementarity at a certain level can be expected to increase an organization's comparative advantage, the firm will actively pursue technologies and organizational reforms for achieving that level. Compaq and others have developed a series of devices in the production of personal computers, such as the modularization of production and the outsourcing and standardization of parts, intended to decrease the need for coordination between task units within the firm, thus allowing the company to use its resources more effectively by concentrating them in a few of its stronger areas. In the past, the degree of corporate integration under the functional hierarchy of the typical American firm was quite high; its wide-ranging application of outsourcing was first induced by studying and applying the subcontracting system used by Japanese companies. However, by initially accepting IBM's specifications on the one hand, and making manufacturing data publicly available on the other, the emergent American computer companies expanded their supplier networks to include geographically distant and historically unrelated suppliers. By opening up coordination, which has been kept closed among *keiretsu* firms in Japan, they were able to decrease their costs even further.

In addition, American organizational evolution toward the differentiation of systemic information intensified the competition between firms in processing information on the systemic environment extending beyond the boundaries of the individual firm. This interfirm competition will contribute to the development of system standards for newly emerging industries such as the Internet industry. In these kinds of fields, the USA exhibits an advantage that cannot be matched by Japanese-style organizations.

One would be rash, though, to look only at American leadership in the information and digital communications technologies (ICT) and conclude that Japanese-style organizations are experiencing an overall decline. Rather, the horizontal hierarchy, in which collective information processing is complemented by individuated information processing, has the potential to function as a sophisticated organizational mode in industries that still require continuous coordination between specialized skills. Consider the traditional examples of the automobile and machine tools industries, which were developed by combining electronics and machine technologies. Once the standards of the ICT markets become clearly delineated, several Japanese companies are likely to rise quickly to the forefront of the manufacturing side of that industry. In fact, technological complementarity already exists between the ICT industry and the advanced machine tools industry. Technological innovations in computer graphics are making it possible to achieve ultra-precision manufacturing technology at the molecular level, referred to as nano-technology; and new materials at the elemental level, in turn, are likely to have an impact on the ICT industries. However, the future of Japanese firms in these kinds of fields is going to depend on the modification of their assimilated information structures, which in the past have been closed to all but the enterprise or the enterprise group, by accommodating more open outside transactions with parts suppliers and other partners. As stated above, several American manufacturing firms have reworked and improved their functional organizations. In their turn, Japanese firms now have to study and implement the use of interfirm communications, supply, and development networks employed in America's differentiated information structures, in an attempt to achieve revitalization in the information age.

On the other hand, once the assembly of automobile and consumer electronics becomes standardized, manufacturing firms will gain the classical comparative advantage in terms of low land and labor costs by moving their manufacturing bases to emerging economies. This does not necessarily mean the hollowing out of the manufacturing industry, however, because the late developers do not yet have the comparative advantage in the development of machine tools needed for manufacturing. Also, as we saw in the last chapter, economies like China have not yet solved the core institutional problem of designing a corporate governance structure that can effectively manage its relatively cheap labor. Until credible corporate legal reforms are introduced, the advanced nations, including Japan, will hesitate to jump wholeheartedly into China.

Naturally, the movement of manufacturing bases from Japan overseas will create new problems. Feedback to the development team from the manufacturing site might be cut off, and this could compromise the development capabilities of the horizontal hierarchies in Japanese firms. However, this may not necessarily suggest a flaw in the horizontal hierarchy itself, but simply raises the question of how to extend that hierarchy over a wider geographical space. Digital communications technologies will surely be relevant to finding a solution to this dilemma.

Let us say that in the Asia Pacific region a complementary relationship in industrial strength exists between Japan and the USA. The USA continues to be the leader in developing industrial concepts, such as network techniques and new financial instruments. Japan has carved out its own niche in upgrading manufacturing technologies (high engineering). China is striving to take full advantage of its latecomer status to selectively introduce institutions and technologies from Japan and the USA, and to take advantage of its large market and inexpensive labor pool. Economic gains from this kind of mutual interdependence on a global scale could not be realized if all economies were to converge toward a single model, because this complementarity arises from the combination of organizational diversity between Japan and the USA, with China's comparative advantage in the classical dimensions.

Can the economic gains from diversity be fully realized through free trade? The next section looks again at the evolutionary model presented in Chapter 3 to approach this question analytically.

CAN THE ECONOMIC GAINS FROM DIVERSITY BE REALIZED THROUGH FREE TRADE?[3]

Let us assume that the world consists of two nations, the (large) A-economy and the (small) J-economy, and that the economies only contain two industries, the M-industry (multimedia/communications) and the V-industry (VCRs), the products of which can be traded. Suppose an organizational convention has developed in the A-economy, for example a functional hierarchy sustained by functional skills, or its evolved form, the decentralized hierarchy, and that both industries are organized on the basis of this convention (differentiated information structure). Also assume that organizational innovation (i.e. the introduction of a horizontal hierarchy through the evolution of contextual skills) for improving the productivity of the V-industry has been implemented in the J-economy, but that its organizational mode is inferior to the decentralized hierarchy in the M-industry.

At this point, assume hypothetically that the J-economy and A-economy are economically integrated in the following sense. According to the evolutionary game framework for organization formation presented in Chapter 3, the populations of the A- and J-economies are integrated, and their members are randomly matched. Because the percentage of J-nationals is assumed to be small, this corresponds to the situation in

---

[3] Aoki, "Organizational Conventions."

which contextual skills and the organizational mode based on those skills will eventually be eliminated by the evolutionary pressures of Darwinian dynamics. A rather loose interpretation of these results may lead to the following conclusion. If foreign direct investment (FDI) is liberalized, an organizational innovation in a small nation will be eradicated if special efforts are not made by innovative firms to recruit and train personnel to perpetuate that reform. Otherwise, new workers entering the workforce will view their employment potential at innovative firms as relatively low, and will choose the safe investment in functional skills over an investment in contextual skills. As a result, the organizational mode of innovative firms will be impossible to maintain.

Thus, the small J-economy may try to protect its organizational innovation by regulating the inflow of production factors from other countries or regulating foreign direct investment. Suppose trade is completely liberalized, however, and the prices for products from the V-industry and the M-industry would be determined through competition on the international market. Also suppose that consumer preferences in both countries are identical, and that all consumers spend about half of their income on each of these two products. That is, the price elasticity for demand of both products is one. In this case, Darwinian dynamics will prompt J-economy nationals to invest in contextual skill formation and enter the V-industry in which those skills have the comparative advantage, and to leave the M-industry in which those skills have the comparative disadvantage. Eventually, the market for M-industry products in the J-economy will be supported by imports from the A-economy.

This has interesting implications. The J-economy now specializes in the V-industry, in which it has the comparative advantage, but it cannot completely fulfill worldwide demand because of its small size. Thus, product prices will be set at a level at which the V-industry in the A-economy, which does not have the absolute advantage, is sustainable – in other words, at the level at which the V-industry and M-industry in A-economy, under a differentiated information structure, would be able to produce the same level of profit. This means that the V-industry in the J-economy, which achieved an organizational innovation and was protected against the threat of foreign direct investment, can acquire a kind of differential rent, that is a "quasi-rent," from that economy's organizational innovation.

Figure 7 depicts the expected payoffs of economic agents in both economies and the potential for quasi-rents under free trade. (Sample figures from Chapter 3 were used to create this diagram.) Line u^J represents the expected payoffs of economic agents in the J-economy, line u^A

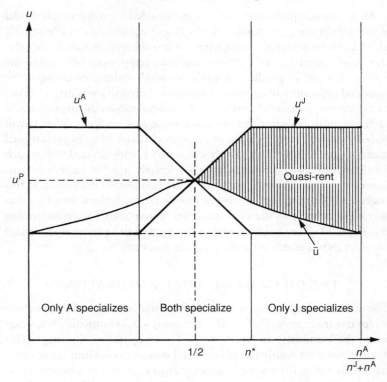

Fig. 7 Free trade and quasi-rent

represents the expected payoffs of economic agents in the A-economy, and line $\bar{u}$ represents the average expected payoffs of agents weighted by the size of the populations. The ratio of the A-economy's population size n^A to the J-economy's population size n^J is shown on the horizontal axis. When the J-economy is small relative to the A-economy, it is initially positioned toward the right. Until the supply size of the A-economy drops below a certain threshold n^*, the economic agents in the smaller J-economy, which has carved out a niche in the V-industry, will monopolize the gains from free trade. Once the relative size of the A-economy crosses the threshold n^*, the A-economy will withdraw from the V-industry in which it has the comparative disadvantage, and will begin to reap the economic gains from the international diversity of organizations by specializing in the industry in which it has the comparative advantage, the M-industry.

An important implication that can be extracted from this simple model is that maximum gains from diversity (the P-equilibrium in Chapter 3), u^P, will only be achieved through free trade if the relative size, or the relative supply capability, of the two economies happens to be equal to the ratio of demand for products from the M- and V-industries. Owing to the bounded rationality of agents, organizational diversity was first achieved by the development of different organizational modes as conventions in each economy. However, the optimal economic gains from diversity will only be derived from free trade by chance. Gains from organizational diversity can be fully realized only if diversity is endogenized within each economy, or if two economies that are relatively equal in size but heterogeneous in organizational convention are completely integrated. Is this really possible, in spite of the inertia toward an institutional structure that is complementary to the organizational convention? Before addressing this issue, let us revise the model in this section to be more realistic and consider its implications for the Japanese economy.

THE DILEMMA OF "BUREAUPLURALISM"

The model in the previous section assumed that as soon as the opportunity for free trade arose, the "small" J-economy would immediately specialize in the V-industry in which it had the comparative advantage. This assumption is obviously unrealistic. Just because an economy is not internationally competitive in a particular industry, given that economy's prevailing skill type, it does not mean that the industry will be completely eradicated by international competition. Contextual skills especially will be devoid of economic value outside the industry in which they were formed because they are unique to a particular organization. Accordingly, agents equipped with those skills will demand protection from international competition in the industries in which they do not have the comparative advantage.

The result of providing protection to comparatively disadvantaged industries is that the J-economy will not specialize in the V-industry in which it has the comparative advantage, and the amount of quasi-rent it can acquire through free trade will decrease. Nonetheless, if the efficiency achieved in the V-industry through the evolution of contextual skills is sufficiently high by international standards, it may be possible for the J-economy to accrue a certain amount of quasi-rent unattainable by other economies. This rent may be shared with workers in the underdeveloped M-industry through the protection mechanisms such as import regulation.

The acquisition of the quasi-rent will begin to decline rapidly, however, if the foreign exchange surpluses acquired by the J-economy as a result of protected trade are invested in the A-economy and the organizational innovations in the V-industry are transplanted there, or if the international demand for V-industry products declines because of an appreciation of J-currency. At this point, the ability of the V-industry to subsidize the underdeveloped M-industry will decline; unless firms in the comparatively disadvantaged M-industry exit, or unless there are innovations that introduce the organizational mode with the absolute advantage in that industry, the V-industry itself will cease to be internationally competitive. The implications of this model are extremely suggestive of the contemporary Japanese economy.

Thus far in this book I have explained how the effective management of Japanese firm organization that endogenizes contextual skill formation has been supported by the complementarity of the contingent governance structure and the imperfect labor market. The contingent governance structure in turn has been supported by regulations restricting entry to the banking industry which have made it possible for main banks to accrue rents. More generally speaking, the regulation of entry into an industry and the protection of weak firms in disadvantaged industries has been one of the primary institutional elements sustaining the Japanese economy. By committing to the protection of the human capital value of the specific skills formed in each industry, they have provided economic agents with incentives to invest in contextual skills. In Japan, most working people in all fields have been expecting the value of their human capital to be maintained through a multilayered structure comprising their employing firm, the industrial associations in their industry, and the ministry that oversees that industry. In my book published in 1988, this system was referred to as "bureaupluralism."[4] The term "bureau" originally referred to a "drawer" and implied sorting or arranging something. The bureaucracy has played an important role as agent and arbitrator in protecting the vested interests of pluralistic groups in different fields.

However, "bureaupluralism" is not an "open pluralism" as vested interests protected by bureaucratic administrative mediations merely coexist

---

[4] Masahiko Aoki, *Information, Incentives and Bargaining in the Japanese Economy*, Cambridge: Cambridge University Press, 1988, ch. 7.

and various organizational modes cannot be freely created. This joint gain by all parties was made possible by the existence of quasi-rents acquired from the international market by upgrading the machine manufacturing industry, which accounts for 80 percent of exports. It was maintained by distributing the quasi-rents attained by the internationally advanced sectors to the underdeveloped sectors through such mechanisms as domestic price distortion, taxes and subsidies, and entrance regulations.

However, if organizational innovations in manufacturing and development achieved by advanced sectors like the machinery industry become stylized, they can be learned by firms in other industrialized countries, and can then be transplanted to developing countries. If the learning or transplantation of these organizational innovations is combined with low cost factors of production overseas, the potential for the Japanese economy to acquire quasi-rents will rapidly decline. This trend will be further accelerated by organizational innovations or the emergence of new industries in other countries. In a previous work I referred to the following phenomenon as the "fundamental dilemma of bureaupluralism": advanced sectors that do not need bureaucratic protection tend to drift away from the bureaupluralistic framework, while less developed sectors tend to rely on it more.[5] As long as the acquisition of quasi-rents from the international market by the former is possible, the size of the pie that can be distributed among interest groups will expand, so that the maintenance of bureaupluralism will not be especially problematic. It may even contribute to social stabilization. However, if quasi-rents move toward extinction for the various reasons given above, the framework of bureaupluralism itself will be difficult to maintain. At this stage, if comparatively disadvantaged industries seek continued protection, the advanced firms would either lose their competitiveness due to higher subsidization to disadvantageous sectors and interest groups, or would be forced to move their manufacturing bases overseas to survive. The resulting dilemma would be that the only remaining employment opportunities would be in comparatively disadvantaged industries.

FROM BUREAUPLURALISM TO OPEN PLURALISM

The assessment of the Japanese economy presented in this chapter is ambivalent. I have argued that, from the perspective of information

---

[5] Masahiko Aoki, ch. 7.

processing, there is potential for the economy to continue to demonstrate efficiency in industries that can be characterized as high engineering industries. There is also a fairly high possibility that new innovations will be implemented domestically in cross-industrial technologies, such as information-technology-driven electronic machinery, retail and service sector networking, and environmental management technologies. I also pointed out, however, that "the dilemma of bureaupluralism" might grow more serious, threatening the loss of international competitiveness of the leading industries. Is there a way to resolve this dilemma?

The combined effect of such factors as the bounded rationality of individuals, evolutionary pressures, and institutional complementarity is a tendency for a more or less homogeneous organizational convention to be adopted throughout a particular economy. However, different organizational conventions will evolve in different nations. This is an unintended outcome of the workings of bounded rationality. This chapter has made it clear that the potential gains from organizational diversity cannot be fully realized on a global scale merely through free trade. This is a proposition that stands even if we assume a purely theoretical situation in which all resources can be traded and there are no costs involved in transportation, storage, etc. If we acknowledge the existence of resources or services that cannot be traded, the proposition gains even more credence.

In Ricardian classical trade theory, the primary source of comparative advantage within an economy is the relative quantities of the "primary factors of production" – land, labor, and capital – which cannot themselves be moved between countries. The world can enjoy the gains of trade by first converting these factors of production into outputs that can be traded. What has been emphasized here, however, is that a world comprised of boundedly rational individuals can reap economic gains because of the diversity of "organizational modes," a human construct. Theoretically, these could have been constructed by human intent anywhere, at any time.

As everyone knows, however, establishing a new organizational mode different from the prevailing convention is not an easy task, regardless of whether it is a creative innovation or a transplant from outside. The skill types needed to sustain a new organizational mode may not be readily available in the economy, and the institutional structure supporting the existing organizational mode may not be conducive to experimentation with mutant modes. This places an exceptionally heavy burden on the Japanese economy, where bureaupluralism has been implemented, because tall barriers have been constructed to obstruct new entrants. By contrast, economies whose official regulatory stance is to allow free entry into industries, such as under the Anglo-American system, have institutional structures that are more tolerant of experimentation with mutant organizational modes.

Not only is it unrealistic, therefore, to try to remodel the Japanese economy on the Anglo-American system, but it would be counterproductive to the pursuit of economic gains from diversity. As suggested by the sample figures in Chapter 3, the transition costs of attempting to realize the gains from diversity (P-equilibrium) via the circuitous route of shifting the Japanese-type of organizational equilibrium (J-equilibrium) toward the Anglo-American-type of organizational equilibrium (A-equilibrium) would be excessively high. In terms of lowering transition costs, it would be more efficient to try to realize the gains from organizational diversity by incorporating the beneficial aspects of the functional or decentralized hierarchical structure of organization into the Japanese-type of organizational equilibrium (the J-equilibrium).

Accordingly, permanently solving the dilemma of bureaupluralism requires institutional reform that allows new organizational modes to be experimented with and implemented in industries where the conventional assimilated information structure is inefficient. There is no guarantee that the Japanese-type of horizontal hierarchy will maintain an absolute advantage in the industries in which it was originally an organizational innovation. The operations of a self-sufficient horizontal hierarchy may be especially inefficient in fields in which strategic alliances between various firms can be expected, like the communications industry. In these fields, the relevant systemic environment extends across several industries, and processing information regarding that environment may require a greater breadth of information processing capabilities than can be accumulated by a single firm. However, it is not yet altogether clear which organizational mode is most suitable for these industries. In the USA, firms are experimenting with various organizational modes and strategic alliances premised on information differentiation. Adaptable organizations will be evolutionarily selected through the process of experimentation and competition. This being the case, the framework of bureaupluralism should be revised to allow organizational experimentation even in industries in which Japan holds the comparative competitive advantage.

Bureaupluralism is by nature resistant to institutional reforms that threaten the vested interests of certain interest groups, making it politi-cally difficult to carry out drastic institutional reforms. However, as has already been shown, bureaupluralism cannot be sustained, as the quasi-rents are inevitably eliminated by the maturation of that pluralism itself and by changes in the international environment. As has been repeatedly emphasized, attempts to sustain it would only result in the loss of com-paratively advantaged industries. Thus, the only tenable choice remaining is to look for a new path to economic gains by lowering barriers in all industries and allowing the entry of diverse organizational modes from both domestic and foreign sources. The time has come for the Japanese people to make the painstaking efforts needed to endogenize the economic gains from diversity.

GOVERNANCE OF DIVERSITY: LIFTING THE BAN ON PURE HOLDING COMPANIES

It is easy to argue in favor of the economic gains from diversity and the relaxation of market entry regulations for realizing them. As has been stated repeatedly here, however, a structure of formal and informal insti-tutions evolves in an economy to effectively maintain a certain organiza-tional convention. Consequently, it is not possible for the elimination of some institution or regulation to result in the immediate formation of a new organizational mode, or for diversity to suddenly be realized. The creation of diversity itself requires the formation of new regulatory struc-tures, private arrangements, and informal customs. Also, as we saw for transition economies in Chapter 6, attempts to transplant institutional structures far removed from a particular economy's historical constraints will be hard-pressed to survive the internal evolutionary process.

Let us look once again at why suboptimal multiple equilibria emerge in the evolutionary game based on random matching, as formularized in Chapter 3. If a player adopts an alternative to the socially prevalent strat-egy (skill formation), that player will risk having to pay the high costs of mismatching. Thus, it is in the best interests of the boundedly rational player to choose the socially prevalent strategy. If, however, the prob-ability of proper matching is high even if the player does not choose the socially prevalent strategy, the sustainability of mutant organiza-tional modes will increase, eventually resulting in an equilibrium where diverse organizational modes are used in different industries. The first to suggest the implications of this local matching were Robert Boyer and André Orléan of the French Regulation School.[6] The creation of a governance structure that would intervene in and motivate the combination of nonprevalent skill types would help make this "local" matching possible.

I would like to use this final section to advocate the abolition of the ban on the pure holding company system in Japan from this theoretical perspective.[7] Corporate governance structures are determined individually by each firm within a framework of legal constraints. Accordingly, if the legal prohibition were to be lifted within the framework of bureaupluralism, it would be voluntarily adopted in places where such a choice was desirable. But how could the introduction of pure holding companies help make it possible to implement selective organizational change such that the horizontal hierarchy would be preserved in organizations where it had performed well in the past, and replaced by other organizational modes in organizations where it had exhibited inferior performance?

Pure holding companies were eliminated in the process of dismantling the *zaibatsu*, and their abolition was legally ratified by Article 9 of the Anti-Monopoly Law of 1947. Made possible only by the special circumstances of Japan's defeat followed by the postwar occupation, this prohibitive regulation was a rarity. The law permitted the possession of business-related subsidiaries only by business holding companies, that is companies that operated a particular business by themselves. Why has it now become desirable to lift the ban on pure holding companies, a ban that has not been considered problematic thus far? In other words, what can pure holding companies do that business holding companies cannot do, particularly in the contemporary Japanese context?

In a business holding company, the strategy unit and company business units are contained in the organizational framework of a single company. This organizational scheme was not initially problematic in the stages of economic development in which strategic decisions regarding moves into new businesses were influenced by the industrial policy decisions made at the national level through the intervention of the Ministry of International Trade and Industry (MITI). Nor was it problematic later, when

---

[6] Robert Boyer and André Orléan, "Persistence et changement des conventions: Deux modéles simples et quelques illustrations," in André Orléan (ed.), *Analyse économique des conventions*, Paris: Presses Universitaires de France, 1994, pp. 219–48.

[7] The prohibition against pure holding companies was repealed under a revision to the Anti-Monopoly Act that went into effect in December 1997, about three years after this book was written. [Added in translation.]

firms competed for efficiency through the evolution of their own horizontal hierarchies. In fact, it could be considered efficient for achieving continuous product development and organizational innovations/technological improvements in the manufacturing process. Until that time, many presidents of manufacturing companies were recruited from either the personnel department of the company's headquarters, or the engineering or sales departments of the firm, depending on the comparative strength of the company. The personal, psychological, and informational proximity between on-site workers and top executives was highly conducive to the horizontal hierarchical mode of organization, which utilized a feedback loop in which on-site information regarding the market or manufacturing was fed back to those making the strategic decisions regarding product development or business diversification. The systematic management of human resources in firm organization, such as employee appointments, transfers, and promotions, were undoubtedly of strategic importance in supporting the human side of the Japanese-style of organization principled on information assimilation. The nature of the on-site proximity style of business management may continue to be effective in certain industries and lines of business. The problem, however, is that current regulations prohibiting pure holding companies force that organizational mode on all firms equally. What kind of problems might arise as a result?

One problem is that flexibility in strategic thinking and breadth of perspective tend to be sacrificed if the strategic decision-making unit is too close to the work site. The president may be too preoccupied with the market performance of a new product from his former department, or may be compelled to take responsibility for a defective product. As the speed of technological innovations and market development accelerates, as international competition intensifies, and as cross-industrial and international strategic corporate alliances and the buying and selling of corporate assets become increasingly important in deciding strategic corporate policies, those responsible for strategic decision making will need to do their thinking at a certain distance from everyday business operations. Maintaining this distance, however, is quite difficult in organizations that have evolved on the principle of information assimilation. We are no longer living in an era in which MITI can engage in strategic decision making on the behalf of firms. For example, when making decisions to expand into industries like ICT, where industrial standards have not yet been clearly developed, the coexistence of and competition between decentralized and varied strategic decision making at the level of the firm can be expected to have inherent advantage in terms of the perspective of system evolution. Unilateral government control inevitably causes information assimilation among firms, and heightens the social costs of errors. Further, at the level of the firm, the strategic decision-making unit and business divisions must operate as separate organizational units, with some degree of distance between them.

Turning all business divisions into equal subsidiaries may help eliminate discriminatory distinctions between business divisions integrated with the parent firm and those of the firm's subsidiaries. This would not only be useful in eliminating domestic and foreign managerial distinctions arising in the face of the increasing weight placed on the business of overseas subsidiaries, but may also compensate for some of the deficiencies of the assimilated information structure of organization without sacrificing its benefits. As I mentioned in Chapter 2, the assimilated information structure is information-efficient when there is strong complementarity between tasks and when close coordination of tasks is required. Internal resources will not be used effectively under this system, however, when there is resource competition between tasks. Also, in the formative periods of new industries, or when engaging in development activities characterized by high uncertainty, it is desirable for different actions based on differentiated information to be selected through the evolutionary process of natural selection. For example, some companies in the communications industry may pursue a strategy of developing wireless, satellite-based digital communications. The future of the communications industry, however, may in fact lie in the expansion of cabled computer networks. Simultaneously pursuing these divergent possibilities, however, is very difficult for an organization operating on the basis of information assimilation. It will be easier for a parent company to undertake alternative business projects that compete with each other by forming separate subsidiaries or joint ventures.

This also makes it hard to ignore criticisms that the recently introduced deregulatory measures regarding the establishment of securities subsidiaries by banks remain incomplete, as these measures generate the same problems as business holding companies. When the main bank system functioned effectively, the framework that established barriers between the banking and securities industries was, as seen in Chapter 5, consistent as a regulatory framework. However, as firms have become more and more independent of banks, and bond issuance has become a main source of long-term funding for well performing companies, it has become desirable for the banking and securities industries to compete on the same playing field so that the less fit institution can be weeded out through natural selection. This explains the desirability of institutional reform measures that would integrate the banking, securities, and trust subsidiaries under financial holding companies. Such integration would have been effective for the evolutionary redistribution of the human resources for monitoring, which had been concentrated in banks. However, the creation of securities subsidiaries by banks might give parent banks incentives to keep the securities industry in a secondary position.

The second argument in favor of separating the parent company functions from the business divisions concerns personnel management. Under the business holding company system, the parent company internalizes business divisions that institutionalize a fairly rigid personnel management structure in terms of salaries, promotions, pensions, and bonuses. By making the employee–firm relationship permanent, these systems have contributed to the formation of the contextual skills needed in the operation of a horizontal hierarchy. However, the institutionalization of these systems also makes it difficult to implement an annual salary contract system, merit-based compensation, or skill-based contract differentiation. The real reason that Japanese business corporations establish so many subsidiaries and rely on subcontractors is often that they want to implement a system of personnel management that differs from the rigidified personnel system of the parent company. As a result, however, tasks that should be integrated end up getting divided between the parent company, its subsidiaries, and its subcontractors. One of the merits of a pure holding company is that turning business divisions into equal subsidiaries allows for the differentiation of personnel management systems. That is, if each subsidiary can choose a mode of personnel management based on its own business and labor situation, the merits of the conventional "Japanese-style" employment system can be maintained whenever useful, even as diversity in employment arrangements is gradually institutionalized.

The development of pure holding companies would also contribute to the effective use of specialized skills. Knowledge and skills in fields such as finance, international negotiation, law, and the assessment of new technologies can quickly become outdated in today's international business environment. However, the effective use of young professionals with specialized skills who have the most recent training in these fields is thwarted by the homogeneous seniority-based wage system used under the business holding company system. If a pure holding company system is adopted, perhaps employees with specialized knowledge, as parent company staff, can be treated under a different salary structure from the one used in the business divisions. Later, when the peak productivity of those employees' specialized knowledge has passed, they can be transferred to management positions in one of the company's subsidiaries, and effectively rerouted back into the conventional Japanese employment system.

The third reason for rescinding the ban on pure holding companies is financial. As previously stated, a cloud is hovering over firm monitoring by main banks due to the firms' declining reliance on bank loans. Managers who do not rely on bank loans are almost entirely free from external monitoring. Many crimes and scandals committed by managers during the Bubble period went unchecked because of a lack of external monitoring. One of the functions of a pure holding company is to monitor managers of business subsidiaries through financial control. By observing the regular cash flow of a subsidiary, the monitor may detect financial problems sooner. If the parent company staff is able to intervene when a subsidiary falls into financial distress, then contingent governance will have been internalized within the firm.

The final question is, who is going to monitor the pure holding company? The Fair Trade Commission is concerned that lifting the ban on pure holding companies will invite international criticism regarding their potential for strengthening the financial *keiretsu* and, though it has not said so explicitly, for reviving the *zaibatsu*. However, lifting the ban on holding companies would probably not compel today's gigantic business corporations, which operate over a wide range of fields, to operate under the umbrella of a single pure holding company. It is unlikely that the management corps of the larger firms would voluntarily forfeit their de facto corporate control rights in this manner. Even in the USA, where the market for corporate control is fully developed, there are clear examples of conglomerates that cannot function effectively as corporate governance structures. If those forms of economic control were to become a real threat, they would surely be checked by anti-monopoly regulations.

Consequently, the most likely result of lifting the ban on holding companies is that existing business corporations would spin off their business divisions into subsidiaries. Also, related firms might merge to establish a parent company, with each individual firm surviving as a subsidiary. In either case, there would not be a very great difference between the parent company's stockholding structure and that of the current business corporation. Thus, it would also be unrealistic to expect the market for corporate control to emerge to monitor parent companies. As was already noted in Chapter 4, even the market for corporate control in the USA, where it is fully developed, is rapidly losing its effectiveness as a primary mechanism for corporate monitoring.

This being the case, the remaining option is to assign existing institutional investors, that is, the principal shareholders, or banks, life insurance companies, and auditors, a more active monitoring responsibility than they have exercised in the past. Rescinding the ban on pure holding companies would require that corporate laws be revised, for example to impose strict standards on the disclosure of subsidiary balance sheets, to require that at least one third of the board of directors are outsiders, to assign strict fiduciary duties to those directors, and so on.

Another function that might be expected of the pure holding company is the provision of venture financing. The ex ante monitoring capabilities of Japanese banks tend toward the assessment of managerial and organizational skills of firms with which they have had longstanding relationships, and, as already noted in Chapter 5, these skills are lagging far behind American venture capitalists in terms of amassing the technological assessment capabilities needed for considering venture firm financing. It goes without saying that securities firms are also lacking these capabilities. The party with the greatest ability to assess the latent potential and commercial viability of new technologies in Japan is the business corporations themselves. Pure holding companies may be able to organize these competencies internally or in venture-capital-like subsidiaries if the ban on pure holding companies is lifted and a consolidated corporate tax scheme is simultaneously introduced. If the pure holding company and/or its subsidiaries can fulfill the role of venture financier and support diversity in personnel systems, and if diverse employment contracts can include a term employment contract system for employees with specialized skills, it will become a qualitatively different sub-institution in the institutional structure from that which has sustained the conventional Japanese style of organizational mode thus far. That is, the pure holding company system may be able to function as a framework that offers incentives for specialized, functional skill formation and that mediates flexible combinations and recombinations of those skills through financial measures.

Even if the prohibition against the holding company system is rescinded, it will be up to each firm to decide whether to utilize that system. In this regard, lifting the ban on pure holding companies will clearly be no magic wand for solving the dilemma of bureaupluralism in the Japanese economy. But that is no reason to prohibit them. Besides, it is believed that this will clear a path for moderate yet politically feasible reforms that would help internalize organizational diversity within the Japanese economy. Wavering on the decision to lift the ban on holding companies due to fears of *zaibatsu* revivals or international criticism about the strengthening of the *keiretsu* will do nothing to shelter us from criticism for exhibiting anachronistic attitudes and a lack of international awareness.

Postscript 2000

CHAPTER 1

This chapter was originally meant to be an introduction to a basic line of thought in comparative institutional analysis (CIA) for Japanese readers. Thus, it focuses on CIA's application to the Japan-related topics that follow, but (in retrospect) deals inadequately with its general framework. It refers only cursorily to such important concepts as the path-dependent nature of an economic system, institutional complementarity, relationships between regulations and institutions, institutional change, and so on. At that time I laid down the outline of my thoughts on these issues in the presidential address I delivered at the 1995 annual meeting of Japanese Economic Association; I have included this as an appendix to this English edition.

Regarding the basic issue of what institutions are, there has not been a clear consensus on this among economists. In an analogy of an economic system with a game, some (such as Nelson) identify institutions with players of the game (e.g. prominent organizations such as the government, the central bank, the court, industrial associations[1]), others (such as North and Hurwicz) identify them with the rules of the game,[2] and still others (such as Schotter, Greif, and Young) identify them with the equilibrium outcome or beliefs of the game.[3] I basically adopt the third,

---

[1] Richard Nelson, "The Co-evolution of Technology, Industrial Structure, and Supporting Institutions," *Industrial and Corporate Change*, Vol. 3 (1994), pp. 47–63.

[2] Douglass North, *Institutions, Institutional Change and Economic Performance*, Cambridge, UK, and New York: Cambridge University Press, 1990; Leonid Hurwicz, "Toward a Framework for Analyzing Institutions and Institutional Change," in Samuel Bowles, Hebert Gintis, and Bo Gustafsson (eds.), *Markets and Democracy: Participation, Accountability, and Efficiency*, Cambridge, UK, and New York: Cambridge University Press, 1993, pp. 51–67.

[3] Andrew Schotter, *The Economic Theory of Social Institutions*, Cambridge, UK, and New York: Cambridge University Press, 1981; Avner Greif, "Microtheory and Recent Developments in the Study of Economic Institutions through Economic History," in David Kreps and Kenneth Wallis (eds.), *Advances in Economics and Econometrics: Theory and Applications 2*, Cambridge, UK, and New York: Cambridge University Press, 1997, pp. 79–113; Peyton H. Young, *Individual Strategy and Social Structure: An Evolutionary Theory of Institutions*, Princeton, NJ: Princeton University Press 1998.

institution-as-an-equilibrium, view. There are many merits to this view. For example, it can deal with the issue of enforcement and origins of institutions endogenously. Because of the development of mathematical tools for analyzing the interdependencies of equilibrium choices by the agent within a game, as well as across different domains of a game, we can rigorously deal with the interdependencies of institutions (e.g. institutional complementarity). Regulations, policy decisions, and laws specify the parameters defining the rules of the game, but the equilibrium outcome may be different from the one intended by law-makers and the government. For example, even if the law prohibiting the smuggling of drugs is enacted, if the general practice is to bribe the law enforcers to circumvent it, the law can hardly be regarded as an institution but the practice of bribery can. This insight may provide significant implications for the role of public policy and for an understanding of the mechanism of institutional change. Public policy can influence the equilibrium outcome, and thus the possible formation of an institution, but only via its incentive impacts on the strategic interplay of agents. These and related issues are discussed in a recent article of mine.[4]

There is one important point to be stressed regarding the institution-as-an-equilibrium view. As Alex Field reminded us some time ago,[5] we cannot build a model of a game completely constituted of institution-free, solely technologically determined rules. Some humanly devised rules of the game are already implicitly or explicitly included in any game model. Even if we suppose we can, there would be multiple equilibria. Then we cannot predict endogenously which of those equilibria will be chosen without some other information, such as history, or institutional environments surrounding the domain of the game (institutions existing in surrounding domains). This implies that, in spite of the development of the game theory on which institutional analysis relies, game theory alone cannot provide a complete, closed frame for institutional analysis. The analysis of historical and comparative information must be essentially complementary.[6]

As I said above, I subscribe essentially to the institution-as-an-

[4] Masahiko Aoki, "Institutional Evolution as Punctuated Equilibria," in C. Menard (ed.), *Institutions, Contracts and Organizations: Perspective from New Institutional Economics*, London: Edward Elgar, 2000.

[5] Alex J. Field, "On the Explanation of Rules using Rational Choice Models," *Journal of Economic Issues*, Vol. 13 (1979), pp. 49–72.

[6] For an insightful treatise of such methodology, see A. Greif, *Genoa and the Maghribi Traders: Historical and Comparative Institutional Analysis*, Cambridge, UK, and New York: Cambridge University Press, forthcoming, Part I.

equilibrium view. However, I have begun to think that it is better to refine the view further, as follows. An institution is a shared, self-sustainable, summary expectation held by agents of a way the games are repeatedly played in a certain domain. That is, an institution is a social device to coordinate expectations of the agents in a domain (e.g. market exchange, organizational transaction, polity, commons). In making a choice, the agents cannot know, and do not need to know, every detail of the equilibrium, but need know only a summary representation of its salient features. Thus, regulations, changes in a law, policy, etc., can induce an institutional change only when it can affect the expectations of the agents dramatically. Also, when a taken-for-granted expectation begins to be doubted by the agents, the demise of an institution begins.[7]

CHAPTER 2

This chapter seeks one of the most fundamental sources of competitiveness of the firm, in the informational efficiency of internal coordination schemes – or information systemic architecture. Although such an approach has not been common in economics, I firmly believe that it holds a key for understanding the changing comparative competitiveness of firms, particularly in the age of the information and communications technology revolution. In retrospect, the analytical comparison in Chapter 3 has remained essentially static. However, the framework may be useful for understanding the dynamic informational efficiency of the Silicon Valley phenomena as well. In Chapter 3 the essential feature of the "decentralized hierarchy" was characterized as the scheme in which each task unit separately processes information arising in systemic as well as idiosyncratic environments. In addition, it was assumed that the structure of task decomposition was designed ex ante under managerial leadership, and that each unit is engaged in a non-overlapping task contributing to the well defined organizational objective.

Instead, let us assume that each task corresponds to the development of a modular product in a niche market that could constitute a component of a potential innovation system. However, since a viable and productive system design is highly uncertain, there is no ex ante centralized system design (as in the case of the development of the IBM 360) that specifies tasks of component units, and multiple agents (entrepreneurial firms)

---

[7] Readers who may be interested in further development of such arguments and their implications may wish to consult Masahiko Aoki, *Toward a Comparative Institutional Analysis*, Cambridge, Mass: MIT Press, forthcoming in 2000.

compete in the same niche markets to develop the best modular product (duplicated development efforts). Since their potential products are mutually competitive in a respective niche market and thus are mutually substitutes, in order to win the development race, each entrepreneurial agent needs to "hide" their information processing from the others. On the other hand, as their products can constitute only modular parts of a potential innovation system, the interfaces of their products, the protocol of data and message exchanges between them, needs to be standardized. So there must be a modicum of information sharing among entrepreneurial agents regarding the part of the systemic environment pertaining to these needs. Such sharing of information may be mediated by a third party, such as the venture capitalist, an industry standard-setting association, or an established leader in the relevant niche market. On the other hand, the collection and interpretation of information regarding the systemic environment pertaining to the internal product development is hidden as said, or differentiated. Therefore, this system may be characterized as a variant of a "decentralized hierarchy" discussed in the chapter, although it is the system composed of many autonomous entrepreneurial agents whose tasks are partially overlapping and whose systemic information processing is partially mediated by third parties.

Suppose that, as the information about the systemic environment pertaining to the development of an entire innovative system evolves, the identity of the competing entrepreneurial agent who is ahead in the developmental race in each market may become gradually clearer. It is the essential task of the venture capitalist to pick up the winners ad interim based on the collection of such information and to lead them to the completion of the development projects (say, up to the initial public offering) by additional venture capital financing. The losers must exit without any gains. Thus, an innovative system is formed evolutionarily by the ex post combination of the winners' modular products, rather than by an ex ante centralized design. When there is a large degree of uncertainty regarding the systemic environment, and if the technological complementarity between modular products across niche markets is low, it is clear that the former system will be able to produce a better outcome than the latter. The reduction of technological complementarity can be facilitated by the standardization of interfaces and protocol.

However, there is a cost unique to this system, that is the costs of duplicating development efforts in the process of the development race. Financial and human assets used by losing entrepreneurial agents become deadweight losses from the societal point of view. Against this, if the potential value of winning the race is extremely high, and if the precision of picking the winners by the venture capitalist is believed by competing entrepreneurial agents to be precise, then it can be proved that the social gains from higher efforts elicited from the competing entrepreneurial agents and the flexibility resulting from the ex post combinations of modular products can be high enough to compensate for the deadweight losses.[8]

As noted, the model described here is not that of a coordination scheme internal to a single firm, but rather one among a clustering of entrepreneurial firms and venture capitalists viewed as a system. However, whereas IBM employed hundreds of thousands of engineers at their peak, there are an estimated 7,000 start-up firms in Silicon Valley, each employing only a few or, at most, hundreds. Thus, comparing a large integrated firm from the 1970s and 1980s with a single entrepreneurial firm of today does not make sense. A proper comparison would be between the former and a cluster of the latter. Also, the modeling of the Silicon Valley phenomena as above and the analytical examination of its performance characteristic, specifically its innovation capability in a highly uncertain systemic design in high technology, can also shed light on a unique challenge that the Japanese firms began to face in the 1990s.

CHAPTER 3

In this chapter I tried to show the possibility of the co-evolution of an organizational convention (either J-type or A-type) and an associated human asset type (either contextual or specialized, functional skills) using a simple evolutionary game model. I also hinted that the co-evolution is likely to induce the evolution of various supporting arrangements, such as associated educational and training organizations, industrial relation systems, laws, etc. In order to make the underlying model analytically tractable, I formulated it in such a way that the agents in a homogeneous population strategically select a type of skill and an industry, and that the type of organizational structure is determined only as a

---

[8] See Masahiko Aoki, "Information and Governance of the Silicon Valley Model," in X. Vives (ed.), *Corporate Governance: Theoretical and Empirical Perspectives*, Cambridge (UK): Cambridge University Press, 2000, for the comparison of R&D organizations using a framework similar to the one in this chapter; see *Toward a Comparative Institutional Analysis*, ch. 13, for a more technical treatment.

result of the matching of those agents. It may appear more realistic to assume that there are two populations – a population of entrepreneurs (or firms) who select a type of organizational form and an industry, and one of workers who invest in a type of skill and an industry. It is possible to do this with some technical complications, but little additional insight can be gained by it.

Evolutionary game setups, in which an equilibrium evolves as a result of mimetic actions of the agents, appear to be appropriate for explaining the genesis and sustenance of conventions, norms, traits in skills, preferences, etc.[9] An alternative approach to the institutions-as-an-equilibrium view is the classical repeated game approach using reputation arguments.[10] In this approach an equilibrium is sustained by the ability of the agents to predict precisely what other agents would do even in unrealizable contingencies. Self-sustaining "expectations" become the central defining characteristics of an institution. Normally, the evolutionary game and the classical repeated game approaches are regarded as mutually orthogonal in their presumptions about the rationality of the agents. The former builds on the presumption that the agents are so limited in predictability and rationality that they imitate only the best practice with inertia, while any novelty in strategy choice is regarded as a mutation unexplained in the model. On the other hand, if the latter approach is taken literally, the agents are assumed to be capable of perfect deductive reasoning regarding what other agents will do in any conceivable future contingencies. However, one may argue that the classical game approach tries to capture the characteristic of a state from which agents will have no unilateral incentive to deviate, once established by history. In my opinion, the evolutionary game and classical game approaches are not mutually exclusive, but are complementary to each other in understanding the evolution and self-sustainability of institutions.

One of the most important concepts presented in this chapter is that of

---

[9] Important works along this line include Robert Sugden, *The Economics of Rights, Cooperation and Welfare*, Oxford: Basil Blackwell, 1986; Young, *Individual Strategy and Social Structure*; and Samuel Bowles, *Markets as Cultural Institutions*, forthcoming. For evolutionary thinking, although not explicitly game-theoretic, also see Geoffrey M. Hodgson, *Economics and Evolution*, Ann Arbor: University of Michigan Press, 1993.

[10] Representative works are Greif, "Microtheory and Recent Developments"; Barry Weingast, "The Political Foundations of Democracy and the Rule of Law," *American Political Science Review*, Vol. 91 (1997), pp. 245–63; and Randall L. Calvert, "Rational Actors, Equilibrium, and Social Institutions," in Jack Knight and Itai Sened (eds.), *Explaining Social Institutions*, Ann Arbor: University of Michigan Press, 1997, pp. 57–93.

"institutional complementarity." This concept is developed in the Japanese context in the following two chapters, but, admittedly, this notion may not be defined as clearly as it should be. Since this notion has become casually referred to these days, sometimes without precision, it may be worth reiterating a precise conceptualization here.

Suppose that there are two domains of the games (say, a financial transactions domain and an organizational domain), denoted by $\mathscr{A}$ and $\mathscr{B}$. For simplicity's sake, suppose that the game in each domain is played by a group of agents who choose a strategy from two alternatives. Each agent in domain $\mathscr{A}$ faces the choice between α' and α'', while for each in domain $\mathscr{B}$ the choice is between β' and β''. If every agent in domain $\mathscr{A}$ chooses α' (alternatively α''), an institution A' (respectively A'') evolves in that domain. Likewise, if every agent in $\mathscr{B}$ chooses β' (alternatively β''), an institution B' (respectively B'') evolves in that domain. In each domain agents may or may not have different preferences over alternative institutions. For example, some agents in domain $\mathscr{A}$ may prefer institution A', while the others may prefer A''. Likewise, some agents in domain $\mathscr{B}$ may prefer institution B'', while the others may prefer B'. However, whenever an institution has not emerged (as agents make different choices), every agent assesses that their marginal gains from switching from one choice to another will always increase when any of the other agents do the same switching. (Technically, there is strategic complementarity in each domain.)

Further, let us assume that the agents in each domain are similar in the following weak sense. All the agents in domain $\mathscr{A}$ feel that the "relative" preference for α' over α'' always improves if the prevailing institution in domain $\mathscr{B}$ is B' rather than B''. Likewise, all the agents in domain $\mathscr{B}$ feel that the "relative" preference for β'' over β' always improves, if the prevailing institution in domain $\mathscr{A}$ is A'' rather than A'. Note that these conditions are formulated with respect to "relative" preferences over individual choices, so that some agents may still derive higher utility under A'' (respectively B'). For example, I may have an absolute preference for the worker-ownership arrangement in the organizational domain over the outside-ownership arrangement. But my relative opposition to the latter may be mitigated if efficient and well-regulated markets are functional in the financial domain.

If the conditions just described hold together with the strategic complementarity condition within each domain, then the following holds. (Technically those conditions may be referred to as the supermodularity conditions.[11]) There can be two equilibrium combinations across the two domains, that is two self-enforcing institutional arrangements: A' and B', or A" and B". Then we say A' and B' (alternatively, A" and B") are in institutional complementarity. Both combinations could be possible, even if either of them is Pareto-inferior, that is, even if every agent can be objectively better off in the other arrangement. Such coordination failure can occur because of strategic complementarity as discussed in the text. If one institution, say A', has evolved historically in one domain for some reason, then the institution that is likely to evolve in the other domain is B', even if all the agents could be better off under combination A" and B". How then can the agents coordinate their strategy choices to move from an inferior institutional arrangement to a better one? What role, if any, can public policy play in the transition? These are fundamental questions facing comparative institutional analysis.[12]

CHAPTER 4

In this and the next chapter I discuss how the organizational form of Japanese firms based on information sharing, the so-called lifetime employment system, and the main bank system constituted a coherent overall institutional arrangement as an alternative to the combination of firm organization based on specialized skills and information processing, competitive job markets, and markets for corporate control.[13] As should be clear in the postscript to Chatper 3, saying that a certain overall institutional arrangement exhibits a coherence in the sense of institutional complementarity does not mean that it is inherently efficient in every industry. The relative efficiency property of one arrangement over the others may depend on changing technological and market conditions. Alternatively, they may not be rankable according to the Pareto-welfare criteria.

One more thing to note: I derived the second-best arrangement for team-oriented production, the contingent governance, in an abstract

[11] For supermodularity analysis and games, see Donald Topkis, *Supermodularity and Complementarity*, Princeton: Princeton University Press, 1998; Paul Milgrom and John Roberts, "Rationalizability, Learning, and Equilibrium in Games with Strategic Complementarities," *Econometrica*, Vol. 59 (1990), pp. 1255–77. Also see Aoki, *Toward a Comparative Institutional Analysis*, ch. 8.2 for the following proposition.

[12] See Aoki, *Toward a Comparative Institutional Analysis*, chs. 9 and 10, for this.

[13] In ibid., ch. 11.2, I discuss another type of institutional complementarity surrounding corporate governance: co-determination in the corporate governance domain and national corporatism in the polity domain, as observed in Germany.

setting. As should be clear, the role of the ex post monitor need not necessarily be borne only by a bank. It can be borne by any third party, such as a holding company or a management company. As noted by Michael Jensen, leverage buyout (LBO) partners in the USA simulate the role of the Japanese main bank in its heyday in a manner reminiscent of the contingent governance.[14] This point has bearings on discussions in the postscripts to Chapters 5 and 7.

CHAPTER 5

This chapter is based on the World Bank EDI study on the Japanese main bank system mentioned in the Foreword. It identified the heyday of the system as 1951–75, while recognizing increasing difficulties of the system afterwards when it became more embedded in the competitive global markets. However, after this chapter was written, the currency-cum-banking crisis hit four East Asian economies (Thailand, Malaysia, Indonesia, and South Korea) in 1997. Toward the end of the year, in Japan as well, indecisiveness on the side of both the financial sector and the government regulator in resolving the bad debt problems mounting in the aftermath of the burst Bubble culminated in the bankruptcy of one major city bank and one major securities house. These events triggered an economy-wide credit crunch in Japan, which more than anything else was responsible for the subsequent plunge of the Japanese economy. These crises, in both East Asia and Japan, naturally cast grave doubt on the effectiveness and credibility of the so-called "bank-oriented" financial system *à la* East Asia (or Japan). Immediately after the crisis, some were prompted to declare the inherent supremacy of the "transparent" arm's-length financial system of the Anglo-American type over the opaque, corrupt, relational financial system. When the crises subsided earlier than expected, however, the balance of views seems to have been somewhat restored. The currency and banking crises in the East Asian economies is now being blamed more on a combination of a weakness in the domestic banking sectors with the volatility of short-term capital flows unregulated under the current architectural design of international finance, although the issue of how to cope with the latter remains highly controversial. But what about the Japanese main bank system? Is the system that became entrapped in such a muddle not inherently deficient?

The chapter identified possible merits of the main bank system in its

---

[14] Michael Jensen, "The Eclipse of the Public Corporation," *Harvard Business Review*, Vol. 67(5) (1989), pp. 49–74.

heyday as follows: (1) the provision of a framework for the contingent governance that was complementary to the team-oriented organizational convention; (2) the savings of monitoring costs in the scarcity of specialized monitoring resources; (3) the provision of a safety net for scarce organizational resources in the event of temporal external shocks; and (4) inter-industrial coordination to avoid coordination failure due to the incompleteness of future markets. (Premiss (3) may be subsumed under (1) in the Japanese context, but I keep this premiss separate to consider its implications in a wider context.) It also pointed out that to sustain the system it was necessary for bank rents to be created, and this was accomplished mostly by government regulations in Japan. It was not specifically stated, but could have been, that the framework for the contingent governance of banks was provided by the government – the institutional arrangements generally referred to as the "Convoy System." (Needless to say, banks themselves are firms conventionalizing Japanese practices.[15]) That is, the government played the role of ex post monitor as characterized in the previous chapter vis-à-vis banks. In particular, the expectation that the government is responsible for the control of financially distressed banks, either through bailing-out or an arrangement of acquisition by healthier banks, was generally shared and taken for granted.

When major financial institutions were forced into liquidation at the end of 1997, the taken-for-grantedness of this presumption suddenly came to an end. Even healthier banks reacted to this situation by recalling loans from borrowers who were hit by the credit crisis. This triggered the crystallization of the lingering suspicion among borrowers that banks might not be capable any more of rendering help to distressed borrowers. Such a dramatic reversal in a taken-for-granted belief can indeed be regarded as the end of the main bank system as an institution. (Recall the conceptualization of an institution described in the postscript to Chapter 1.) In retrospect, then, the period between 1975 and 1997 can be seen as one marked by its gradual failure to adapt to increasing environmental changes, particularly the information technology revolution and globalization of financial markets. I consider that a strong institutional complementarity existing in Japan between the form of political economy – what I call "bureaupluralism" in Chapter 7 – and the main bank system is responsible for this failure, to which I will return later (postscript to Chapter 7).

---

[15] Masahiko Aoki, Hugh Patrick, and Paul Sheard, "The Japanese Main Bank System: An Introductory Overview," in M. Aoki and H. Patrick (eds.), *The Japanese Main Bank System*, Oxford: Clarendon Press, 1994, pp. 27–30.

Does the demise of the main bank system in the current context of the Japanese economy, together with the East Asian currency and banking crises, suggest there was a generic problem with relational financing? Should the adoption of more transparent Anglo-American arm's-length financing be recommended everywhere? Of the merits of the main bank system listed above, premiss (1) is certainly Japan-specific to a great extent. Japanese multinational companies have tried to transplant their employment practices and management styles, or at least to create a hybrid of them with indigenous practices, when they have established manufacturing sites abroad, particularly in East and Southeast Asia. However, those practices are still far from conventionalized abroad. If Japanese companies want to institutionalize the frame of the contingent governance of their transplants, they can do so by themselves acting as ex post monitors of them. (Recall the point made in the last paragraph of the postscript to Chapter 4.) Premiss (4) also may not constitute a good reason for relational financing any more in the present context, where global organizations of various types capable of simulating future markets, such as consulting companies, investment banks, and international developmental service organizations, are active. However I contend that premisses (2) and (3) still deserve serious consideration.

Consider premiss (2). In developing economies, most scarce resources may be thought of as information assets, capable of identifying and judging entrepreneurial and managerial qualities, as well as the trustworthiness, of indigenous businesspersons and of monitoring their business conduct. It is precisely their own inability in this respect that led international portfolio investors to make financial deals with the East Asian economies in the form of short-term credits that were recoverable at low costs. But such capacities are often not codifiable and take the form of intangible human assets – "inalienable information assets" (Brynjolfsson) – in the sense that they cannot be easily alienated from the human mind in the form of software, digital data, icons, etc.[16] Note, in fact, that the potentially high economic value of such uncodifiable information assets are not just a unique characteristic of the developing economy: the more digital information is available globally and in real time, the more valuable uncodifiable information of various types may become. A conspicuous example is the venture capitalists, who take in most of the

---

[16] Erik Brynjolfsson, "Information Assets, Technology, and Organization," *Management Science*, Vol. 40 (1994), pp. 1645–62.

funds from institutional investors and refinance only those entrepreneurs active in the physically accessible vicinity for continual face-to-face communications and monitoring. Although the content of inalienable information assets in developing economies is different from that possessed by venture capitalists, as well as banks vis-à-vis small firms in advanced economies, nevertheless, their potential economic value cannot be obviated. From this perspective it cannot be too highly appreciated, other than as a self-serving rhetoric, that international portfolio investors blame only the lack of transparency – that is, the absence of codification of information – of the financial systems of the crisis-stricken economies after the fact, while overlooking their own lack of monitoring competence.[17]

Premiss (3) may also be relevant. With the underdevelopment of financial markets, the default of a major credit contract is likely to trigger chain reactions involving even otherwise healthy businesses. Clearly, it is necessary to put into place an effective mechanism designed explicitly to deal with systemic bankruptcies arising out of large macroeconomic disturbances and to preserve still scarce organizational assets. Here an effective bankruptcy law should play an important role.[18]

In any case, the major problem with the crisis-stricken economy was not the lack of transparency as such, but rather the immaturity of the banking sector, which was incapable of managing effective relational banking based on sound monitoring competence. For example, Yoon Je Cho had pointed out before the Korean crisis[19] that a co-insurance scheme among the government, industries, and banks in Korea fostered a moral hazard of the latter two and made the government captive to a vicious cycle of intervention. This made the banking sector vulnerable to a grave misallocation of financial resources. What, then, is needed for the development of a solid banking sector? Is relational banking possible at all in a market environment far more globally integrated and competitive than in the heyday of the Japanese main bank system?

---

[17] For more on this, see Masahiko Aoki, "A Note on the Role of Banking in Developing Economies in the Aftermath of the East Asian Crisis," paper presented at the First ABCDE–Europe conference of the World Bank in Paris, June 1999.

[18] See a series of works and speeches by Joseph Stiglitz on this subject in relation to the East Asian crisis. e.g. Joseph Stiglitz, "Corporate Bankruptcy, Financial Sector Restructuring and Social Safety Nets" and "The Global Financial Crisis: Perspectives and Politics," Washington, DC: World Bank, 1998.

[19] Yoon Je Cho, "Government Intervention, Rent Distribution, and Economic Development in Korea," in M. Aoki et al. (eds.), *The Role of Government in East Asian Economic Development*, Oxford: Clarendon Press, pp. 208–32.

As emphasized in Chapter 5, bank rents supportive of the emergence and (initial) sustenance of relational banking à la the Japanese main bank system were provided mostly by government regulations in the form of the "financial restraint" and bond issue regulations. A substantial differential was created between the deposit rate and lending rates. Part of the rents created thereby were spilled over to the borrowers. Thus, the Japanese economy was susceptible to the "over-borrowing syndrome," even in the heyday of the main banks system, which had to be held in check periodically by the credit-tightening policy of the government. However, the "over-borrowing syndrome" of the East Asian economies prior to the 1997 crisis was created in the context of open financial markets. McKinnon and Pill[20] explain this as follows. Imagine a developing economy with the domestic deposit rate, i, that is higher than the deposit rate of the same maturity in US dollars, i^*. If there are no barriers to international financial flows and no domestic deposit rate control, competitive market arbitrages will lead the nominal interest rate differential to be equal to the forward exchange rate premium f, so that $i - i^* = f$. If this condition holds in markets (otherwise market arbitrageurs can make unbounded profits without any risk), any bank will be indifferent as to whether to borrow in domestic currency or to accept dollar deposits and at the same time hedge the position in the forward market. Therefore, if banks are required to hedge all their foreign exchange borrowing in the forward market, incentives will not exist for "overborrowing" from international markets by banks and others.

Suppose, however, that there is an expectation among banks that bank deposits will be implicitly guaranteed by the government. This expectation alone would induce the moral hazard behavior of banks that underestimate downside bankruptcy risks. Suppose, further, that the regulatory agency does not impose the 100 percent hedging requirement on domestic banks. The interest rate spread, $i - i^*$, is then explained as the risk premium formed through the interactive estimates by market makers on foreign exchange risk. But this spread may provide incentives for some banks to ignore the risk of bankruptcy and currency devaluation. "Therefore, moral hazard could lead banks to take unhedged foreign exchange positions, borrowing foreign currency to on-lend to domestic residents at much higher interest rates in domestic currency, while implicitly transferring most of the currency risk incurred onto the government through the

---

[20] Ronald McKinnon and Huw Pill, "Exchange Rate Regimes for Emerging Markets: Moral Hazard and International Overborrowing," *Oxford Review of Economic Policy*, forthcoming.

deposit insurance scheme."[21] On the surface, the situation appears to be the same as the financial restraint in the heyday of the Japanese main bank system, but the supply of funds to the East Asian economies in the pre-crisis time was not as stable as domestic savings in Japan. Yet competitive pressures in domestic credit markets forced even traditionally prudent banks to pursue the riskier unhedged strategy, creating domestic booms in those economies.

The boom in investment increased demands for non-tradable inputs such as labor, but the government tried to keep the exchange rate fixed under increasing inflationary pressure. However, an eventual arrival of a downside productivity shock was inevitable. Accordingly, as some episodes of bankruptcy triggered the sentiment in international markets that the boom was almost over, foreign lenders started to call in loans and a downward adjustment in the foreign exchange rate became unavoidable. Speculative attacks around this time amplified the magnitude of foreign exchange adjustment. The banks suffered not only from the defaults of their domestic borrowers, but also from huge capital losses arising from their unhedged foreign exchange exposure. The banks were forced to squeeze lending, and the credit crunch even let healthy projects collapse.

In this parable, the choice of a foreign exchange regime plays a secondary role. McKinnon and Pill argue that, leaving aside obvious "bad" exchange-rate fixes like those observed in Russia and Brazil in 1997–8, the established preference for a flexible exchange rate regime should not be taken for granted. The choice of a foreign exchange regime should be judged by its ability to limit a bank's incentives for overborrowing, since an exchange rate regime cannot obviate the need for prudential regulation of domestic banks against undue risk-taking. They argue that a "good" exchange-rate fix to the US dollar – one that is credible and close to purchasing power parity, may well reduce the foreign exchange risk premium. Since the first-best solution to fully control banks' moral hazard behavior is not possible, then short-term capital controls, such as limiting transactions of domestic currency within domestic markets as Malaysia did after the crisis, may be desirable as a second-best, transitory policy to curb the moral hazard borrowing possibility.

In any case, resorting to a flexible exchange rate regime is not a cure-all medicine. The crucial question remains as to how the development of a sound financial system less prone to moral hazard behavior can be facilitated in the developing economy during intermediate financial develop-

---

[21] Ronald McKinnon and Huw Pill, forthcoming.

ment. As noted before, the processing of uncodifiable information unique to maturity transformation services in the developing economy ought to remain as an essential ingredient, if not an exclusive one, of such a system. Thus, an attempt to transit to an arm's-length financial system once-and-for-all could not be a solution. However, as argued in Chapter 5, some rents need to be provided to healthy banks that can possess inalienable information assets to perform the needed function of maturity transformation. The model by Dinç introduced in the text indicates, however, that such rents may be generated and sustained endogenously without the direct intervention of the government in interest rates or direction of loans. They can be formed either as a sort of insurance premium by borrowing firms for relational financing, or as information rents for the scarce inalienable information assets.[22]

CHAPTER 6

As stated in a note to this chapter, this was drawn from ch. 1 of the World Bank EDI project on *Corporate Governance in Transitional Economies: Insider Control and The Role of Banks*. The book was translated into Chinese and Russian and became the object of frequent references and discussions in China afterwards.[23] After the publication of this book, regrettably, I became somewhat out of touch with the ongoing market transition processes in Russia and China primarily because of time constraints. However, I highly recommend Yingyi Qian's "Institutional Foundations of China's Market Transition,"[24] for a succinct summary and solid theoretical appraisal of China's transitional process from a comparative institutional analytic perspective.

CHAPTER 7

One focus of discussion in this chapter concerns the political economy institution in Japan: what I call "bureaupluralism".[25] The basic logic of its

---

[22] For further discussion of types of rent supportive of relational financing and possible public policy recommendations for banking regulation in developing economies, see Aoki, *Toward a Comparative Institutional Analysis*, ch. 12.2.

[23] For example see *Gaigu* (Reform), April 1996 and May 1997; *Bijiao* (Comparative Economic and Social Systems), May and June 1997; Yifu (Justin) Lin *et al.*, *Sufficient Information and State-Owned Enterprise Reform*, Shanghai: Shanghai Renmin Publishers, 1997.

[24] Yingyi Qian, "Institutional Foundations of China's Market Transition," in *Annual Bank Conference on Development Economics (ABCDE: 1999)*, Washington: World Bank, 2000.

[25] For the historical evolution and more detailed workings of this institution, ch. 7 of M. Aoki, *Information, Incentives and Bargaining* may be consulted.

complementarity with other institutional arrangements in Japan may be briefly summarized as follows. Since the Japanese workers and managers are lifetime employees of a company, they become its stakeholders. The task of management is to strike a balance of interests between the investors and the employees, as well as to assert their collective interests vis-à-vis outside interests: the arrangement that is characterized as micro-corporatism, Obviously, companies in the same industry fiercely compete with each other in markets, but when issues are of a political economy nature companies in the same industry have mutual interests in bargaining collectively. Since they are substitutes in the same markets, bargaining individually only endow them with weaker bargaining power. Thus, in Japan industrial associations evolve as important organizations that are complementary to micro-corporatism. Differing from business associations in national corporatism in continental Europe and Scandinavia that are engaged in collective bargaining with industrial unions, they are the super-structure of micro-corporatism practiced at the individual company level. They represent the interests of stakeholders, including employees, of member companies vis-à-vis outside interests, as well as arbitrating the interests between member firms regarding issues deemed inappropriate to be resolved in the marketplace (e.g. allocation of "voluntary" restraints of automobile exports informally agreed upon between the governments of Japan and the USA).

Bureaupluralism refers to the mechanism in which pluralistic interests are represented and arbitrated on the basis of collusion between an industrial association and a relevant administrative bureau in each industry. Industrial interests are represented and submitted to a relevant bureau by the industrial association in its jurisdiction. Bureaus in turn represent and promote jurisdictional interests in the administrative process (such as budget allocation) of the political economy domain in a way that agrees with their own interests in viability and legitimation. However, this is but a static characterization of bureaupluralism, and it has had rather an interesting dynamic as partially described in this chapter. Bureau-pluralism emerged in the 1950s, first with a dominant coalition between big industrial and financial interests on one hand and economic bureaucrats (Ministry of Finance – MOF – and Ministry of International Trade and Industry – MITI) and politicians on the other. However, throughout the period of high growth in the 1950s and 1960s and onward, bureaupluralism became more and more inclusive, in the sense that interest groups other than big companies acquired effective political economy representations. As time passed, more productive and internationally reputable companies started to drift away from the protection of bureaupluralism.

One of the causes of the late 1980s Bubble may be thought of as a symptom of the "dilemma of bureaupluralism" discussed in Chapter 7. During the 1975 depression in the aftermath of the oil shock inflation, Japanese companies drastically reduced their reliance on bank loans. Together with the liberalization of deposit rate control, the era of financial restraint came to an end. (This is why we characterize the end of the heyday of the main banks system as occurring in 1975.) Subsequently, the MOF partially deregulated foreign exchanges in 1980, which made regulatory control over bond issues meaningless, as companies were able to circumvent the regulation by issuing bonds abroad. At this point, some officials at the MOF considered removing the traditional separation of the banking and securities branches, but the force of bureaupluralism then manifested itself. The securities sector fiercely resisted the attempt, with the help of some politicians. It was also in accord with the interests of the most powerful lobby of the banking industry, i.e. long-term credit banks which were considered to be in an advantageous position with the exclusive issuing privilege of bank debenture. As a result, city banks lost an opportunity to make an inroad into the profitable underwriting business, while traditional securities houses enjoyed huge profits under continuing bureaucratic protection without developing investment banking expertise. Banks were driven to be involved more in the high-risk, high-return real estate business. Thus, the failure of bureaupluralism to adapt to the new global and information technological environment may be considered one of the major, if not the exclusive, sources of the generation of the bubble.

Bureaupluralism is by its nature inert and conservative. The principle of consensus making through politico-bureaucratic bargaining makes any radical departure from the status quo involving the sacrifice of powerful interest groups extremely difficult. This is one of the reasons why I consider it so hard for possible institutional reforms to be initiated in the political economy domain in Japan. Rather, increasing chasms between the changing international, technological and demographic environments on the one hand and existing institutional arrangements on the other may create difficulties for traditional practices, as well as opportunities for new businesses. Micro-level experiments may have more effective impacts on the institutional reform in the Japanese economy. The deregulation of a pure holding company extensively discussed in Chapter 7 is only one of the measures implemented recently in the industrial domain that may facilitate such experiments.[26] There are indeed some promising signs of emergent vigor outside the realm of traditional practices. Certainly, the process of institutional reform in Japan is under way, albeit gradually, and even if its direction is not yet clear.

---

[26] After the deregulation of the pure holding company, a few companies have adopted the organizational scheme, while many traditional firms have announced or contemplated plans in that direction. However, implementation is not yet widespread. The major reason is that the adoption of this organizational structure may mean an increase in corporate tax obligations without the introduction of a consolidation tax scheme. Conservative politicians are slow to recognize the critical importance of such tax reform in particular, and the significance, in general, of micro-experiments, rather than bureaupluralistic protection, for revitalization of the Japanese economy.

APPENDIX

Towards a Comparative Institutional Analysis: Motivations and Some Tentative Theorizing

1. INTRODUCTION

It is only in the past decade or so that a variety of critical comparative institutional issues have risen in international and national policy arenas and that economists have started looking earnestly into those issues by broadening the theoretical perspective of economics. This may indicate that the emergence of a new field, *Comparative Institutional Analysis* (CIA), is brewing. As I will discuss below, the CIA field is co-evolving with Historical Institutional Analysis (HIA) and Transition Economics. All these fields recognize that "institutions matter," and share methodological and analytical orientations and interests in many important ways. In the first half of this paper, I hope to motivate the study of CIA and, in the second half, I present some tentative, general insights, that are suggested by the CIA approach.[1]

Major comparative institutional issues which have recently attracted the keen interest of economists include the following:

1 It has been increasingly recognized that within developed market systems there is a variety of institutional arrangements and that the differences between these may be important in determining national or regional advantage and disadvantage in industrial productivity and international competitiveness. Trade

This paper is a revised version of the Presidential Address delivered at the Annual Meeting of the Japan Association of Economics and Econometrics held at Gakushuin University in Tokyo on September 23–24, 1995. In preparing this paper, I owe much to discussions and dialogues with Serdar Dinç, Avner Greif, Kiminori Matsuyama, Paul Milgrom, Kevin Murdock, Tetsuji Okazaki, Masahiro Okuno-Fujiwara, and Ying-yi Qian over the last few years. I have also benefited from reading Greif's unpublished manuscript (1995). Bo Li provided helpful research assistance and comments on the manuscript. Of course, I am responsible for views expressed in this paper. © Japan Association of Economics and Econometrics 1996. Published by Blackwell Publishers, 108 Cowley Road, Oxford OX4 1JF, UK. Reprinted with permission from vol. 47(1), pp. 1–19.

[1] For HIA and Transitional Economics, there are excellent surveys addressed by Avner Greif, John McMillan and Mathias Dewatripont and Gerald Roland at the 7th World Congress of the Econometric Society.

imbalances between nations have often escalated disputes over institutional differences between trading partners. Do, should, or could institutional arrangements become convergent across economies? Or, is there any gain from diversity? If so, what is the best way of exploiting it?

2 In Eastern Europe the state apparatus of centrally planned economies suddenly collapsed. In spite of initial euphoria, however, the transition to market economies has turned out to be neither trivial, nor automatic through privatization. On the other hand, in China and Vietnam, where the transition has been gradual and the role of the state has been pivotal in designing new market-oriented institutional arrangements, economic performances seem to have excelled those of Eastern European counterparts so far. Can the transition be free from the historical constraint of communist legacies? Have China and Vietnam performed better in terms of economic growth simply because of their relatively lagged developmental stage? Should the transition be made in the Big-Bang manner or by the gradualist approach? In what sequence? If there is a variety of institutional arrangements in market economies, at what model should transitional economies aim as a terminal state?

3 The publication of *The East Asian Miracle: Economic Growth and Public Policy* by the World Bank signalled a new stage of debate on the role of state in particular, and that of institutions in general, in the development process. The report documented various features of institutional arrangements allegedly common to East Asian economies and discussed their possible contributions to the high economic performance of that region relative to other developing regions. Does the East Asian state function as a response to pervasive market failures or rather as a complement to the enhancement of private order institutions which stimulates individual incentives? Is an observable difference in total factor productivity between Japan and other East Asian economies attributable to a difference in institutional infrastructure? Is it true that East Asian bureaucracies are less susceptible to unproductive rent-seeking behaviour? If so, why? Are East Asian institutional arrangements only effective at the developmental stage and should they be eventually replaced by a more advanced, universalistic model of Western type?[2]

Although I have quoted above partial, representative institutional issues drawn from advanced market economies, transitional economies, and developing economies respectively, it is immediately clear that they are partially overlapped and should not be analysed in complete independence from each other. I also argue below that they cannot be satisfactorily dealt with by the deductive approach of neoclassical economics and that they call for a new, interactive CIA approach which combines comparative information across various economies with context-specific micro modelling based on recently developed game theory, contract theory, and information economics.

---

[2] For a summary of current issues see Aoki, Murdock and Okuno-Fujiwara (1995).

2. INSTITUTIONS AND THEIR INTERDEPENDENCIES

On several occasions above, I have referred to "institutional arrangements" in the economy. What are institutions? How are they arranged and interrelated? According to North (1990), "institutions are the rules of the game in a society or, more formally, are the humanly devised constraints that shape human interaction" (p. 3). He argues that such constraints evolve as an outcome of the (political) interplay of self-interest seeking groups. Greif (1994) sees that North's two alternative definitions – rules and constrains – are not quite the same, as the latter is inclusive of the former. He submits that "[g]iven the technologically determined rules of the game, institutions – the non-technological constraints on human interactions – are composed of two interrelated elements: cultural beliefs (how individuals expect others to act in various contingencies) and organizations (the endogenous human constructs that alter the rules of the game and that, whenever applicable, have to be in equilibrium." (p. 943) Hurwicz (1993) gives a functional definition of institution. The role of institution is "restricting the type of mechanisms that is admissible. It is a rule about rules. This means specifying which type of choice domain or of outcome function is admissible . . . However, not all restrictions are candidates for institutions" (pp. 59–60). He argues that restrictions need to be self-enforcing (and discusses a conceptual difficulty associated with this aspect of restriction, to which I shall return later).

There are subtle differences in emphasis and possible analytical implications in the above definitions. However, consensus seems to view institutions as humanly devised constraints on economic interactions or mechanisms which are in some type of equilibrium. Let us accept such conceptualization at this moment without much ado. I will present a more formal, game-theoretic conceptualization of institutions in the second half of the paper.

As humanly devised constraints on economic interactions, we may think of the following devices:

* markets and money
* legal and political framework of the state
* contracts and (private order) organizations
* cultural beliefs and social norms

The markets allow the voluntary exchange of goods (with the intermediary of money) among economic players. For this institution to evolve and function, property rights to economic assets need to be clearly defined and enforced. In many cases they are defined by legal rules. In some situations, however, *de facto* property rights may be created without the intervention of the state. For example, rights to a job may be created by the custom of a workshop (organizational form), but even such *de facto* right may be reinforced by legal ruling to support the custom *ex post*.

Contracts may be enforced by the state, if their contents are simple and their defaults are easily verifiable as in the case of the transfer of property rights to physical goods. However, in many instances, the fulfilment of agreements may not be verifiable by a third party (the court) and needs to be self-enforceable. The Folk Theorem suggests that, if defection can trigger a mechanism of inflicting sanctions on the defector in the future, far-sighted agents may refrain from defecting out of concern not to lose their reputations. Reputational mechanisms in the situation where agents change their partners over time are considered as constituting the basis for social norms. It is often interpreted that the long hand of the future is sufficient for the contract (cooperation) to be self-enforceable. However, this may be misleading. As the social network expands, it may become more efficient to create a formal organization to collect, keep, and make available information about deviant behaviours of agents (Milgrom, North and Weingast 1990) or up-to-date labelling of each individual based on such information (membership, licence, credit card – Kandori 1992). Also, outside options which will be available to possible defectors may be defined by a fabric of outside institutional arrangements. They may include coordinated expectations on the consequences of deviant behaviour (cultural beliefs – Greif 1994), which may reflect past organizational forms. Alternatively, but not unrelatedly, they may be defined by available alternative contracting (e.g. alternative employment contracts) so that there may be strong complementarity among various contracts.

Also, contracts may not be able to specify all possible contingencies relevant to their implementation and they may only specify general rules to be followed. For example, Grossman and Hart (1986) argued that, if that is the case, it is generally the most efficient to ascribe rights to decide on the use of assets in unspecified contingencies (residual rights of control) to the owner of assets. But, if assets in cooperation are diverse and their ownerships are diffusive (as in the case of involving job rights), such a principle cannot specify the organizational mode uniquely. More elaborate, explicit organizational rules may become necessary. Recent experiences in transitional economies (e.g. Poland and China) show that a huge improvement in the performance of un-privatized firms has been brought about without a change in property rights, but by the delegation of authority (McMillan 1995). The organizational design (the delegation of authority) and the property rights allocation cannot be identified, yet there may be some type of correlation between them (Aghion and Tirole 1994).

The brief comments above are intended only to indicate that there may be interdependencies among various institutions: property rights, legal rulings, markets, organizations, contracts, cultural beliefs, and social norms. *What is the nature of these interdependencies?* It is by a difference in perception and analysis in this regard that the emergent CIA is differentiated from the neoclassical approach and partially from New Institutional Economics as well. What has given rise to the CIA is not merely to recognize that "institutions matter."

3. THE MARKET CENTRICISM OF NEOCLASSICAL ECONOMICS

The focus of neoclassical economics is on the market institution. Simply put, other institutions (e.g. cultural factors) are exogenous to the economic system, or they (e.g. the state and organizations) are "substitutes" for the markets when the latter are incomplete or when it is costly to find efficient prices.

Neoclassical economics adopts a deductive approach starting from the presumption of an idealized, generic situation in which property rights for all primary resources and goods are exogenously defined. Technological possibilities for transforming primary resources to final goods are exogenously given by engineering data. Cultural factors may be implicit in the preference (pay-off) function of individual agent. But the preference is also regarded as data. From such suppositions, the well-known Fundamental Welfare Theorem is derived: if competitive markets are created for all goods and primary resources through which property rights to their uses can be voluntarily exchanged, Pareto-efficient outcome will result. This state of Walrasian equilibrium forms the universalistic norm of resource allocation.

If the creation of markets for certain goods is impossible or too costly for technical reasons, alternative institutions will emerge as a substitute. For some, the failure of complete markets to emerge justifies state activism. The state intervention through taxes and subsidies is interpreted as analogous to the creation of quasi-markets which simulate, together with existing markets, the function of a complete set of Walrasian markets.[3]

It was the insight of Coase to regard the emergence of another type of non-market institution, organizations, as contractual arrangements aimed at maximizing efficiency in response to the market's absence or imperfection rather than engineering data. This insight eventually led to the paradigmatic development of contract theory in the last two decades. As discussed below, the theoretical achievements of the principal-agent theory provide CIA with important analytical tools. However, I would also like to note the possible pitfalls of becoming complacent with the present state of principal–agent theory as "the theory of institution."

4. PRINCIPAL–AGENT THEORY

Principal–agent theory aims at understanding institutions as contractual arrangements between the principal and the agent(s) under the condition of asymmetric information. In designing contracts, the principal is constrained by the agents' incentive compatibility condition and participation constraint. The Revelation Principle à la Myerson allows the designer of a contract, without loss of generality, to limit attention to contracts that make it optimal for the agent to be truthful (thus the imposition of the incentive-compatibility condition). The Principle seems innocuous if one examines its formal logic. However, its implicit assumption is that there are no communication costs other than agents' incentives not

---

[3] It is interesting to note that there is no disagreement between the neoclassical economists and their major opponents in the debate on the role of government in the East Asian economy, the developmental state theorists (e.g. Wade), in that the state is viewed as a substitute for markets when the latter fail. The major difference seems to be only that the latter views market failure at the developmental stage as pervasive, while the former views it as limited to a certain restricted sphere. See Aoki, Murdock and Okuno-Fujiwara (1995).

to disclose private information unless there is the provision of information rents. There is no other barrier to the transmission of information. Its institutional implication is that any non-cooperative equilibrium outcome of an arbitrary organization can be replicated by a centralized two-tier structure where agents communicate their entire private information to the principal in exchange for information rents and there is no interaction among agents (Melumad, Mookherjee and Reichelstein 1991).

But it is an obvious fact of reality that most organizations are characterized by multi-layered hierarchies in which real authorities are delegated to agents. Also, agents are engaged in vertical and horizontal side trades of various kinds among themselves (pecuniary and nonpecuniary, implicit and explicit) that are not directly controlled by the principal. In fact, there can be many barriers to communications which are not exclusively attributable to incentives. Private information of agents may take the form of expert knowledge which cannot be fully understood by others lacking the expertise. Some information may not be easily codifiable and cannot be communicated without noise, the reduction of information values, time delay, etc. Bounded rationality of the principal may make it impossible to communicate directly with all agents in the organization without causing excessive information costs. The efficiency of lateral interactions within the framework of principal – agent theory has been investigated by assuming that there is private information among agents which cannot be communicated to the principal (Varian 1990; Holmstrom and Milgrom 1990; Itoh 1992). Under such a situation, allowing side-contracting among agents may become optimal for the principal.

This development of principal–agent theory suggests that optimal organizational design from the viewpoint of incentives may depend on the information structure of the organization (how information is distributed within agents, how efficiently information can be communicated). However, once the bounded rationality of agents is admitted, the information structure of the organization itself may not be technological data. As agents may be limited in their capacity and scope of processing information, organizational design may entail the design of the information structure (what information to be processed by whom and how much – Aoki 1995b) as well as incentive design. The integration of these two aspects of organization is still at an extremely primitive stage of development in economics.

Another apparently innocuous element of principal–agent theory is the participation constraint. However, the outside options of agents may not be completely determined by the market institution alone. In his pathbreaking historical institutional analysis of agency-contracting among Maghribi traders with that of Genoese traders in late medieval overseas trade, Avner Greif (1994) showed how a difference in cultural beliefs conditioned optimal contracting as well as subsequent institutional developments in response to market expansion. He identified cultural beliefs with expectations with respect to the fate of agents who cheated, or more formally, expectations with respect to off-the-path-of-play that constrain on-the-path-of-play behaviour. He distinguished between Maghribis collective value and Genoese individualistic value. In the former the trader expected that the cheater would not be employed by other traders, while in the latter the opposite is the case. The Genoese trade organizations eventually came to dominate, but Greif pointed out that it was not clear that it was because their contracting was more efficient. Contracting based on individualistic value was more adept, however, at responding to expanding markets and generating institutional innovations (e.g., permanent family company).

In the spirit of Holmstrom (1982), Aoki (1994) showed that the moral hazard in teams (organizations) may be controllable by the introduction of a third party who is committed to a menu of interventions – liquidation, rescue, surplus extraction, non-intervention – contingent on observable outcome jointly determined by team efforts and stochastic events. Such third-party intervention becomes more effective in controlling moral hazard in teams, the lower the outside option value for team members is in the event of liquidation. An implication of this is that it is complementary to the third-party monitoring scheme that organizations are mutually formed as teams and the workers are not mobile across different teams without losing their potential value. Further, incentives for the third party to commit itself to the contingent action menu need to be provided. It should properly be engaged in applying sanctions when necessary, while it should not abuse its right to punish.

An example of the theoretical construct of the third-party-monitoring scheme is main banks in Japan. It has been suggested that an implicit contract arrangement among main banks to mutually delegate monitoring responsibilities, together with a regulatory framework to assure rents to main banks for the fulfilment of their responsibility, may provide an institutional framework for the main banks neither to be too soft nor too hard in monitoring (Aoki and Patrick 1994).

This and previous examples suggest that the effectiveness of contracts and organizations is supported by a fabric of institutions which define outside options for organizational participants and constrain individual and organizational behaviour. The organizational (contractual) environment may consist not only of markets, but also other parallel or superimposed organizations, as well as cultural beliefs. A corollary of this observation is that at present it is desirable to accumulate context-specific models for a deeper understanding of the function of institutions. Specifically, it seems necessary to make the assumptions on information constraints of organizations and outside participation constraints more explicit, based on comparative information. The present state of contract theory is far from generating a general theory of institutions, even if such a thing may potentially exist. By accumulating context-specific models and testing their predictions in the light of comparative evidence, we may gradually advance in understanding the nature of the interrelatedness of various institutions, and thus that of economic systems in general.

5. FAILURE OF NEOCLASSICAL DEDUCTIVE APPROACH

Recently a serious public policy failure of the deductive approach of neoclassical economics became evident in the area of transition economics. When the communist political regimes in Eastern European economies collapsed in the early 1990s, the high hope was that their economies would be able to convert to market economies à la Walras by quickly privatizing property rights in productive assets. It was expected that if the state-owned enterprises were privatized, then a market for shares in the privatized corporation would quickly emerge as an effective monitoring mechanism for its management. However, as soon as the initial euphoria over the sudden demise of authoritarian regimes subdued, it turned out that the transition to market economies was not so trivial a matter.

The transition involves three facets: the initial condition or the legacy of the communist regime; the terminal target – what type of market system should be targeted; and the process for moving from the former to the latter, e.g. sequencing, speed of transition, etc. The neoclassical advocates perceived the Walrasian norm as the target and insisted that the best route for achieving this was to escape from the initial condition as soon as possible by the Big Bang approach.

However, the political reality of the communist legacy seemed to have made such an approach untenable. Toward the dusk of the communist regime, the central planner had already yielded much of the authority for economic management to the director of the state-owned enterprise. The workers had acquired vested interests in their enterprise in terms of job security and other economic and social benefits including housing, pensions, health and child care, holidays and recreational facilities, kiosks, etc. Privatization of the state-owned enterprise was not possible without making political compromises with these insider vested interests, unless there were a powerful privatization agency as in former East Germany. Fearful of the possibility that the property rights to the privatizing enterprise would be captured by the ex-planning bureaucrats, reformist privatization agencies were also ready to make such compromise (Boycko *et al.* 1993). The result was the emergence of "insider control" of privatized enterprise: the directors of the former state-owned enterprises gained the majority rights in privatized corporations, in collusion with middle managers and workers (Aoki and Kim 1995). They became virtually free from capital market control except for possible bankruptcy. Even this possibility is mitigated by continued state subsidy disguised as credits.

The Chinese authority which has observed the development of insider control in Eastern Europe is proceeding more cautiously in the transition to a market economy. Instead of aiming at developing securities markets as a means of controlling enterprises, it consciously tries to nurture the development of a commercial banking system by reforming state-owned ex-specialized banks and allowing the gradual entry of new banks. On the other hand, it has been proposed to decentralize the asset management of state-owned enterprises to decentralized state-asset controlling agencies (including enterprises, the ministerial level holding companies and the provincial level holding companies), depending on the size of enterprise (Chinese Government – World Bank Conference 1995, particularly the paper by Q. Jian). These approaches are intended to depart gradually from the initial constraint of state-controlled economy and move towards the market economy, but the final target is not yet clearly envisioned even by reforming administrators.[4]

The Chinese approach may be criticized as ad hoc, slow, ambiguous, etc. However, her economic performance in terms of economic growth per capita compares favourably with that of her Eastern European counterparts. In contrast to the radical, deductive approach in Eastern Europe which was doomed to fail by its inconsistency with the historical constraints of the transition, however, the gradual, inductive approach of China may allow for evolutionary selection among various experiments, e.g. joint ventures with foreign companies, township and village enterprises, partial spinning-off or gradual privatization of subsidiaries by the state-owned enterprises, which are coexistent with initial constraints. We do not know yet whether or not they will succeed in the transition. However, their experimental approach and its relative success may be sufficient to cast a doubt on the universal validity of the neoclassical deductive approach toward policy making.

6. NEW INSTITUTIONAL ECONOMICS

If, as neoclassical economics presupposes, institutions other than markets emerge only as substitutes for efficiency-maximizing markets, every economy would tend to converge to an ideal Walrasian type as a result of competitive selection. However, as I noted at the beginning of this paper, there are many examples indicating that this is not likely to be the case. Why do different institutional arrangements emerge in each economy? Why do inefficient institutions remain? These questions have been earnestly pursued by New Institutional Economics (NIE) under the intellectual leadership of D. North.

In contrast to the neoclassical economics which views non-market institutions, such as the state and organizations, as substitutes for markets, NIE considers that the state may play a complementary role in enhancing market institutions, or may prevent their development because of its own interests. As trade opportunities expand, technologies develop and populations grow, gains from exchange may be better exploited by complementary changes in laws and regulations defining and enforcing property rights. Property rights may be defined and redefined through the interplay of the state, its bureaucracy and various organizations, i.e. through "political markets." The existing allocation of property rights defines transaction costs, and thus players' incentives to exchange, acquire knowledge and innovate, and ultimately promote institutional changes. Institutional changes, the essence of which is changes in property-right definition and allocations, can be brought

---

[4] Deng Xiao-ping described the process as "crossing the river by exploring stones" (mozhe shitou guo he).

about endogenously through the equilibrating process in political markets. However, an economy may be also locked into an inefficient institutional arrangement due to sunk cost in existing institutions and network externalities among institutions. Also the same factors can explain distinct historical trajectories of institutional development and economic growth for different economies.

I consider that NIE has made a major contribution in bringing issues of institutions to the forefront of economics, especially in clarifying the path-dependent nature of institutional development, interdependencies (complementarity) of various institutions, the nature of political structure as providing foundations for market institutions (rather than the substitute for the latter), etc. However, I should like to register a tentative reservation as regards its view that institutional arrangements are basically politically determined. This view seems to be related to North's distinction between institutions and organizations. According to North, "[a] crucial distinction . . . is made between institutions and organizations . . . Conceptually, what must be clearly differentiated are the rules from the players. The purpose of the rules is to define the game as played. But the objective of the team within the set of rules is to win the game – by a combination of skills, strategy, and coordination; by fair means and sometimes by foul means. Modelling the strategies and the skills of the team as it develops is a separate process from modelling the creation, evolution, consequences of the rules" (1990: 4–5).

I will argue later that organization forms may also emerge as a human device restricting and enforcing individual player's admissible strategy domains, i.e. as an institution. However, once organizational forms evolve as such, organizations may become a part of the set of players in the game actually played in the economy. Thus, the dual aspects of organizations as institutions and players are conceptually reconcilable (I formalize this later.) However, my reservation is more substantial. I submit that there are cases when the spontaneous evolution of a private order organizational form is an important driving force of institutional change, triggering complementary changes in the nature of other institutional arrangements. A notable comparative study by Saxenian (1994) on why Silicon Valley is flourishing today after the severe downturn of the early 1980s while Route 128 continues to decline may be read from this perspective. I present my case in relation to a current debate on the nature of contemporary Japanese institutional arrangements. The case may appear idiosyncratic. However, the CIA is aiming at accumulating comparative information before presenting a sweeping general theorizing which fits only a subset of economic systems. As such, my argument may be also interpreted as a rebuttal of the neoclassical paradigm with the Walrasian equilibrium state as the universalistic norm.

7. ARE JAPANESE INSTITUTIONAL ARRANGEMENTS AN ABERRATION FROM THE NEOCLASSICAL NORM?

The impact of state intervention in Japan during wartime (1939–45) on subsequent institutional evolution are now well documented by economic historians

(Nakamura, Hara, Teranishi, and Okazaki among others). An emergent consensus view in the Japanese public forum seems to be that institutions which prevailed during the post-war high growth period and are still prevailing had their origins in war (Okazaki and Okuno-Fujiwara 1994; Noguchi 1995).[5] However, it seems to me that the controversy still remains regarding the nature of subsequent institutional development and its implications for present public policy debate. Is it, as Noguchi (1995) seems to argue, that the prevailing institutional arrangement is just the artifice of the wartime regime (what he calls the "1940s regime") and should be regarded as an aberration from the laissez-faire regime (the neoclassical norm)?

One may consider à la North that a series of state actions, such as replacing stockholders' rights in the corporation with bureaucratic intervention in corporate governance, the introduction of the designated banking system and the organization of industrial control associations as planning intermediaries, was aimed at reducing transaction costs for the bureaucracy to implement war-economy planning. Such measures were initially in serious conflict with the property rights of large capitalists and their managers. Their introduction was made possible only by the extraordinary political power of the military and associated bureaucrats at that time. However, as Okazaki (1987) convincingly argued, the objective of the military–bureaucracy alliance to reduce the transaction costs of war-economy planning did not materialize, not simply because of the destruction of productive assets and the critical shortage of resources but largely because of the overriding costs of sacrificing price incentives for managers. Then, why is it that an institutional arrangement created for the purpose of centralized control seems to have survived up to the present time? Is it simply because bureaucrats have compromised with the private incentives of managers? This is a puzzle to which those who subscribe to the theory of the 1940s regime must find an answer.

My own hypothetical argument may be summarized as follows: in parallel with and subsequent to the centralization efforts by the state bureaucracy, there was spontaneous evolution in private work organizations and the institutional arrangements introduced by the wartime government were transformed in their function to the one which fits this private sector evolution after the war. (I elaborate this theme in a recent article (1995c).)

Although it is becoming increasingly popular to regard the behaviour of Japanese firms in the 1920s in markets for products, labour, and capital as conforming to the neoclassical norm, I suspect that their internal organizations at that time were still far from conventionalized. Many firms retained classical authoritarian hierarchies in which the boss ordered and the workers obeyed. Some government-run model factories, as in steel and shipbuilding, recruited German engineers to

---

[5] I also argued (1988: 184–6) that some aspects of postwar Japanese "arbitrative" management originated in the prewar and wartime periods. But my argument placed more emphasis on the evolutionary nature of institutional changes rather than state actions, the point which I would like to amplify below.

train the workers, but their engineering approach was often at odds with the indigenous craft-oriented approach of the workers to learning. Some paternalistic capitalist firms were tolerant of less authoritarian industrial relationships, allowing more team-oriented work organization. In the sense that diverse work organizations coexisted and no convention had evolved, the situation was "far from equilibrium". The contemporaneous situation in the USA was similar, except that scientific management based on formal job classification schemes was being widely experimented with on a wider scale in advanced industries such as public utilities and financing.

It was during the war that the tendency toward an organizational convention began to occur in both economies, but on different trajectories. In Japan the labour administration perceived that authoritarian hierarchies were not conducive to productive efficiency under the extreme labour shortage that made the threat of discharge an ineffective discipline. In order to enhance workers' morale at strategically important plants the government sponsored the Industrial Patriotic Society movement. The movement was responsible for reducing status differentials between the boss and the subordinates, the white-collar workers and the blue-collar workers, while placing severe peer pressure on the workers to maximize effort. Because of the shortage of materials and tools, emergencies on the shop floor had to be met by the collective improvisation of the workers. In this way, the evolution of a collective approach to work organization was triggered.

It was with the same objective of increasing war production that the US labour administration sponsored the spread of the scientific labour management movement and the job classification scheme in manufacturing industries during the war (Baron *et al.* 1986). Thus, from positions far removed from equilibria, the bifurcation of organizational convention began to emerge: the collective scheme in Japan and the specialization scheme in the USA. As I analysed elsewhere (Aoki 1995b), the managements of each economy mutually learned from the accomplishment of the other at various phases of postwar development when they perceived critical productivity disadvantage vis-à-vis the other. They also refined the respective schemes by organizational and engineering innovations as well as by relying on improved information processing capacity of the workers. However, the bifurcate trajectories seem to have retained distinctive characteristics.

It is my contention that the institutional arrangements initially introduced by the wartime Japanese government became viable in the postwar period by finding fits, after their democratic transformation, with the evolutionary trajectory of private work organizations. The removal of shareholders' control made it possible for the workers to gain shares in property rights in their firms in terms of job security, accumulation of retirement benefits, opportunities to advance to managerial positions. Their position in the firm as stakeholders provides incentives to invest in team-oriented skills. The potential moral hazard of "insider control" is effectively checked by the prospect of bank intervention contingent on the bad performance of teams (Aoki 1994). The industrial association puts peer discipline on member firms not to recruit workers from employees of other member firms, which enhanced the effectiveness of the threat of bank discipline on badly performing firms by reducing outside option values for the workers. On the other hand, the industrial association acted as an intermediary to protect property rights of the stakeholders of member firms vis-à-vis outsiders and feed their interests into the bureaucratic process of industrial policy-making and budget allocations.

The differences between my view and the emergent theory of the "1940s" regime are as follows. The latter claims that prevailing institutional arrangements were created by the state as substitutes for markets and are an aberration from the neoclassical norm previously existing. An obvious public policy implication of this view is to revert to the neoclassical market-supremacy norm. In contrast, I submit that team-oriented work organization began to emerge at the same time as the sweeping institutional changes were introduced by the government in the sphere of finance, corporate governance and industrial associations. The last of these were initially intended as substitutes for markets, but that aim failed. The reason that they have outlived the wartime economy was that they gradually evolved as complementary institution arrangements for subsequent private organizational innovations on the trajectory initially laid out during the war. Although the fit was not an intended one, the government-induced institutions and private order organizational forms together came to form a coherent system, exhibiting competitive advantage in certain industries. Because of its coherence, however, the system is difficult to change in a piecemeal way, even if it seems to start losing consistency with emerging configuration of technological and market parameters. On the other hand, adaptive institutional change will be likely to come only along its own evolutionary path rather than as a jump towards the neoclassical norm.

8. STATE OF PLAY

Let me summarize the points made so far. By inductive reasoning, I submitted a critique on both the neoclassical approach, which views non-market institutions as substitutes for markets, and on NIE, which attaches secondary importance to private-order institutions such as organization forms. An implied proposition is that various institutions, such as property rights and markets, contracts and organizations, cultural norms and beliefs, are interdependent, mutually substitutable or complementary, shaping or shaped. They, as a whole, form a coherent system of self-enforceable constraints on economic behaviour as far as exogenous technological parameters remain within certain admissible ranges.

Once a coherent set of institutional arrangements is regarded as a system, its diversity is easily recognizable. CIA is an emergent field which tries to understand why there is a *variety of institutional arrangements across economies and what are the public policy implications of the diversity.* Is the diversity only a transitory departure from the uniformity? Is it brought about merely by the inefficient deterrence of competitive selection process by elements of monopoly, state coercive power, "irrational" cultural factors, etc.? Or, alternatively, is it understood as representing some kind of multiple equilibria? If so, how is a distinct equilibrium selected in each economy? Should institutional arrangements be made uniform to benefit from competition on a level playing field? Or can there be any potential gains from the diversity?

Obviously these questions cannot be answered overnight. They can be tackled only by gradually accumulating rich comparative information and submitting it for analysis. In order to avoid the pitfall of the inductive approach leading to a premature general theorizing about institutions, CIA adopts an interactive approach combining comparative information and "context specific micro modelling" using game theory, information economics, and contract theory. The assumptions of models should be based on comparative and historical information, and their predictions should be confronted with comparative and historical evidences.

9. DIFFERENCES BETWEEN CIA AND THE NEOCLASSICAL APPROACH

CIA is an infant field and it can hardly be said to signal the emergence of a new paradigm. However, to highlight its possible differences from the market-centric neoclassical approach, I venture to list a few tentative general insights which have been generated or suggested by the interactive CIA approach and submit them for possible refutation.

9.1 Institutions as equilibria

The fundamental nature of institutions is systemic and sustainable constraints on types of admissible strategic choices of players (including human deviced organizations) approximate to equilibrium strategies of a game played in the economy. Institutions may serve to reduce costs of information, implementation, and enforcement, as well as costs of disequilibrium imposed by mutants. Since they approximate to equilibrium strategies, the institutional arrangements of an economic system are self-enforceable.

Games are defined by a set of players and rules specifying for each player a strategy set and a pay-off function defined on the product of strategy sets of all the players. Let us call a game with the following property an original game: players are composed only of individual persons, and strategy sets and pay-off functions are inclusive of all technologically feasible possibilities. The original game may yet be devoid of social structuring. A structure to the original game is provided by restricting the types of admissible strategy domain for each player (for the moment let us suppose that restrictions are exogenous). Such constraints may be self-enforceable among the original players, if they share cultural beliefs, social norms. Or, constraints must be enforced by "the third party" (e.g. the court), or by the creation of an "organization" which can alter the technologically determined pay-off functions for the original players (e.g. the state, financial institutions, labour unions). In the latter case the original game is modified to one (derivative game) defined by an augmented set of players composed of individual persons and organizations, endogenously determined rules on strategy domain and pay-off function for each players (Hurwicz 1993). In either case, the restriction on the original game can become self-enforceable and thus viable only when equilibrium strategies of underlying games, original or derivative, fall within the restriction.[6] When they do, we may call the restrictions *institutions*.

The next question is whether equilibrium is unique relative to exogenous technological parameters. If so, institutions can be interpreted as endogenously determined by exogenous parameters alone and we can have a closed game theory of institutions. However, the next proposition asserts that is not likely to be the case.

9.2 Multiplicity of equilibria

Even for the same exogenous parameters, equilibrium of games is likely to be multiple. Thus a diversity of institutional arrangements is possible.

In the Darwinian learning model of choice of skill type by Aoki (1993, 1995a) and that of coordination game by Matsui and Okuno-Fujiwara (1994), multiple equilibria arise because of strategic complementarity in random matching games played by bounded-rational players. Different equilibria may be supported by different organizational forms (conventions) or cultural norms respectively. In the repeated-game model of financial contracting by Dinç (1995), the sustainability of both relational banking and arm's length banking arises for a certain range of parameter values because of strategic complementarity between entrepreneurs and investors. In Greif (1994), collective cultural belief and individualistic cultural belief, as expectations with respect to off-the-path-of-play that constrained on-the-path-of-play behaviour, are both sustainable and support the two distinct contracting arrangements between traders and their overseas agents in the context of medieval trade.

In the randomized Darwinian dynamic models of Kandori, Mailath and Rob (1993) and Young (1994), continual mutations occurring at the individual level with a very small probability will assure the long-run stochastic convergence of repeated coordination games to risk-dominant equilibrium. However, in large-scale social games, mutations may be controlled by institutionalizing (locally

---

[6] This notion of self-enforceability of institutions distinguishes our approach from Schotter's. According to him, "A social institution is a regularity in social behavior that is agreed to by all members of society, specifies behavior in recurrent situations, and is either self-policed or policed by some external authority" (1981). He identifies a social institution with the von Neumann–Morgenstern concept of a solution in a cooperative game. Therefore the existence of external enforcer is exogenous and the problem of what mechanism makes the enforcer's commitment credible is left unexplained. Further, as Hurwicz argues, the cooperative game solution is a set of outcomes determined partly by the rule of the game (partly by technology) and not the rule itself.

stable) equilibrium strategies as endogenous rules of games (or rules in "stronger sense" than an established pattern of behaviour – (Sugden 1989). Thus, a diversity of economic institutions may not disappear.

9.3 Equilibrium selection, institutional complementarity and institutional path dependence

We need some exogenous factor other than technological parameters to explain the selection of an equilibrium. The economic system as a cluster of institutions may be difficult to change in a piecemeal fashion because of complementarity existing among element institutions. Also an institution may become sustainable because of sunk costs, even if initial factors allowing for its emergence subsequently disappear.

I indicated that the usual technological parameters alone cannot endogenously determine the selection of institutional arrangements. An additional structuring factor is necessary (Field 1981).[7] In the model of Darwinian dynamics by Aoki (1993, 1995a) involving imperfect expectational coordination among entrepreneurs, the dynamic adjustment path bifurcates à la Krugman-Matsuyama at "far from equilibria." At far from equilibria, the dynamic path may go either to a Pareto superior equilibrium or a Pareto inferior equilibrium. There is nothing in the model which can explain path selection except for "pure accident." It is because of this uncertainty that the deductive neoclassical approach cannot provide a complete theory of institutions and we must consider how they start to evolve. In that sense, CIA and HIA (historical institutional analysis) are complementary.

Once an equilibrium is selected and has become institutionalized, it is difficult for the economy to jump to another equilibrium. Playing equilibrium strategies are made implicit or explicit rules of games. Information channels to sustain the equilibrium strategies are sunk as organizational capital (David 1992). When institutional arrangements reflect equilibrium strategies which are mutually complementary, element institutions also become mutually complementary. I term such phenomena *institutional complementarity*.

Aoki (1994) analysed complementarity existing in the Japanese system between employment contracting and financial contracting. The former is characterized by its implicit long-term employment, while the latter involves the contingent governance structure in which corporate control automatically shifts between the

---

[7] Incidentally, Field (1981) criticized the game-theoretic equilibrium characterization of institutions by saying that it is only a variant of neoclassical theory of institutions which in vain tries to explain the selection of institutions by exogenous technological parameters alone. However, as noted already, equilibria may be multiple due to bounded rationality (evolutionary games), differences in expectation with respect to off the path-of-play contingencies (Greif), increasing returns, strategic complementarity, etc. Further, those equilibria may not be Pareto-rankable as we will see presently. Thus, the game theory of institutions cannot be identified with the neoclassical theory of institutions which views existing institutions as efficient response to exogenous parameters. This distinction is clearly made by Nelson (1995). However, as a traditional evolutionary theorist he recorded "uneasiness" with the game theoretic equilibrium concept of institutions (p. 81).

insiders and the main bank contingent on the financial state of the corporation. Even if the long-term employment contract is not efficient for certain technological parameters, contracts of another type may not be viable unless a complementary financial contract also coevolves.

Dinç (1995) showed in the model referred to above that the possibility of relational banking contracts emerging over arm's length banking contracts becomes greater if the amount of bond market financing is repressed, say by regulation. However, once relational banks are established, at least some of them will survive even if the bond markets are deregulated afterwards or the economy is integrated with competitive foreign bond markets. The reason is that reputational costs are already sunk by the relational banks while the sunk costs deter a new entry to relational banking.

Freeman (1995) argued that the welfare state in Nordic economies is a tightly knit system composed of complementary institutional elements, such as high income tax regimes and comprehensive state-run welfare programmes, supportive government regulations of markets, and social partner centralized bargaining agreements. Using an analogy from Kauffman's model of rugged fitness landscapes (the so-called NK model), he suggests that under the condition of strong complementarity it is difficult to improve matters by making a single change or local adaptation, but "long jumps are more important in achieving good outcomes" (p. 20).

It is true that it is not easy to change a coherent system locally. However, it is not yet settled whether "long jumps" are necessary all at once, or whether they can be induced by a strategic move, which may be local, but will trigger chain reactions in other spheres by the very reason of dynamic complementarity. The intensive debate in transitional economics over the similar issue of Big-Bang approach vs. gradualism is neatly surveyed by Dewatripont and Roland (1995).

9.4 Non-optimality of institutional arrangements

Since exogenous parameters do not uniquely determine the selection of equilibrium (thus institutional arrangement), there is no guarantee that institutional arrangements are efficient or converge to an efficient one. The relative efficiency of various institutions depends on the value of exogenous parameters.

In Aoki (1993, 1995a), two distinct organizational forms can emerge in different economies as a result of the strategic choice of agents over types of skill to be invested in. If the majority of agents are committed to investing in skills useful in the specific context of an organization, the type of organization that relies on collective efforts of the workers may become more viable. But the workers make such a commitment only if the organizational type has become conventionalized in the economy. On the other hand, if the workers have invested in specialized functional skills, the type of reorganization that relies on the functional division of tasks may become more viable. But the workers will invest in that way only if this organizational type has become conventionalized. Within organizations, information tends to be assimilated in the former type and differentiated in the latter type. The relative efficiency of the two organizational types depends on technological parameters of industry, such as complementarity and stochastic correlation among tasks within the organization, and neither of them has absolute advantage (Aoki 1995b).

More generally, the relative economic success of (particular sectors in) particular economies at a particular point of time may be generated not by the intrinsic superiority of their institutional arrangements but by the extent to which their path-dependent institutional arrangements are efficient for a particular configuration of exogenous factors at that particular time. For example, the productivity gain of the Japanese automobile firms in the 1980s did not imply the superiority of the Japanese system as a whole, while the innovative edge of American information technology in the 1990s does not necessarily imply the inherent superiority of the American system in all other respects (e.g. the poor provision of safety nets for the disadvantaged).

9.5 Gains from cross-economy institutional diversity

Since a universalistic institutional arrangement (e.g. neoclassical complete markets) which is optimal for any configuration of exogenous parameters is not viable, there are synchronic and diachronic gains from a diversity of institutional arrangements.

Again, according to Aoki (1993, 1995a), the relative efficiency of two organizational forms, assimilated and differentiated information structure, implies that organizational conventions may become a source of comparative advantage to nations (Krugman and Obstfeld 1994) or regions (Saxenian 1994). However, when an organizational innovation which has absolute advantage in some industry occurs in a small economy, the gains from trade may exclusively accrue to that economy as quasi-rents. When two economies of relatively equal size internalizing different conventions engage in trade, both of them may benefit from diversity by mutually specializing in advantageous industries. The gains are not complete (except for accidental configuration of exogenous parameters) in comparison with the case where the optimal organizational diversity can be internalized in each economy. However, it is not easy to see how a diversity of organizational conventions can be internalized in one economy as each convention may have to be supported by a matrix of complementary institutions (such as labour markets, financial systems, regulations, etc.).

As noted above, the shift from one equilibrium to another is not easy, but the cost of transition measured in terms of the necessary minimum size of mutants to upset the old equilibrium will be reduced if the productivity gap between the two equilibria can be enlarged. This suggests that the perception of a large productivity gap with a relatively more advanced foreign convention or innovations may trigger a successful organizational change based on emulation. In reality, however, experiments based on emulation and learning are likely to lead to the modification of the old convention rather than a complete transition to the new convention.

On the organizational dynamic paths of the USA and Japan in the last fifty years, external shock-induced organizational evolutions are evident (Aoki 1995b). Japan's perception of lagged productivity gap in the 1950s and learning of American scientific management method eventually ignited a collective, path-dependent organizational innovation of quality and inventory control. The resulting increased productivity of the Japanese assembly industry provided a reciprocal shock to American industry in the late 1970s and 1980s. America's own conceptualization of Japanese organizational innovation as the "lean production method," combined with its own technological innovation in communications and information technology, led to the rise of new network-based coordination beyond the legal boundaries of corporations, providing a new competitive edge in high technology industry. In turn, Japan seems to be perceiving the widening productivity gap as an alarming demonstration of the urgency of overhauling the prevailing institutional arrangement. Whatever the outcome of evolving experiments may be, its nature may be predicted as path-dependent, however.

9.6 Linkage of different games

When the system moves from an equilibrium of a (derivative) game to another equilibrium (of a possibly different derivative game), expectations crystallized as a part of equilibrium strategies in the former may provide a focal point for the selection of new equilibrium or the initial condition in a dynamic adjustment process through which a new equilibrium is reached (Greif, 1995).

Institutional changes, i.e. changes from one (derivative) game to another, have not yet been analysed in game theory, but this proposition is intuitive and supported by some of Greif's own historical analysis. Although it is not explicitly game-theoretic, Qian and Xu (1993) analyze how differences in coordination mode between planning regimes in the USSR and China may affect the speed, effectiveness, and mode of transition to a market economy. In the USSR, planning was coordinated through centralized ministerial hierarchies organized on a functional (industrial) basis, whereas in China coordination tended to be decentralized on a geographical basis in a locally integrated manner. Regional decentralization in Communist China was deliberately pursued as Mao's strategy to thwart possible disaster that might be inflicted by external attack. This Communist legacy seems to make the gradualist transition in China viable as well as to foster the development of a more decentralized market economy.

10. CONCLUSION

In this paper, the neoclassical deductive approach to institutions has been challenged. It has been suggested that, in order to understand the nature and public policy implications of diverse institutional arrangements across economies, it is desirable to adopt the comparative, interactive approach by which comparative information is accumulated, context-specific models are constructed and analyzed, and their predictions are confronted with comparative evidence.

Some recent work on these lines has been overviewed. One of the insights gained from these works is that the relationship between markets and other institutions, including legal rulings, contracts and organizations, cultural beliefs and norms, is not necessarily that of simple substitute, but may be understood as reflecting equilibrium strategies in underlying economic games. For a given configuration of parameter values, there may well be multiple equilibria, leading to a diversity of institutional arrangements across economies. Distinct institutional arrangements have evolved because of the path-dependent nature of equilibrium selection, and they may not necessarily be Pareto-rankable. It was suggested that there may be gains from a diversity of institutional arrangements. However, these insights are as yet only tentative.

The CIA approach needs to be developed much further before it can provide a sensible guide for a number of important public policy issues. I hope that this paper will stimulate the interests of economists of the younger generation in this infant, yet promising, new field.

REFERENCES

Aghion, P. and J. Tirole (1994) "Formal and Real Authorities in Organizations," mimeo, IDEI, Toulouse.

Aoki, M. (1988) *Information, Incentives and Bargaining in the Japanese Economy*, Cambridge: Cambridge University Press.

—— (1993) "Organizational Conventions and the Gains from Diversity: an Evolutionary Game Approach," mimeo, Stanford University.

—— (1994) "The Contingent Governance of Teams: Analysis of Institutional Complementarity," *International Economic Review*, Vol. 35, pp. 657–76.

—— (1995a) *Keizai Sisutemu no Shinka to Tagensei* (An Evolving Diversity of Economic System), Tokyo: Toyo-Keizai Shinposha.

—— (1995b) "An Evolving Diversity of Organizational Mode and its Implications for Transitional Economies," to appear in *Journal of the Japanese and International Economies*.

—— (1995c) "Unintended Fit," mimeo, Stanford University.

—— and H. Kim (eds.) (1995) *Corporate Governance in Transition Economy: Insider Control and the Role of the Banks*, Washington: World Bank.

—— K. Murdock and M. Okuno-Fujiwara (1995) "Beyond the East Asian Miracle: Introducing the Market-enhancing View," introductory chapter to M. Aoki, H-K. Kim and M. Okuno-Fujiwara, eds., *The Role of Government in East Asian Economic Development: Comparative Institutional Analysis*, Oxford: Clarendon Press, 1996.

—— and H. Patrick (eds.) (1994) *The Japanese Main Bank System: its Relevance for Developing and Transforming Economies*, Oxford: Oxford University Press.

Baron, J. N., F. R. Dobbin and P. Devereaux (1986) "War and Peace: The Evolution of Modern Personnel Administration in US Industry," *American Journal of Sociology*, Vol. 9, pp. 350–83.

Boycko, M., A. Shleifer and R. W. Vishny (1993) "Privatizing Russia," *Brookings Paper on Economic Activity*, Vol. 2, pp. 139–92.

Chinese Government and the World Bank (1995) *Beijing Conference on Enterprise Reform*, Beijing.

Coase, R. (1938) "The Nature of the Firm," *Economica*, Vol. 4 (NS), pp. 386–405.

David, P. (1992) "Why are Institutions the 'Carriers of History'?" SITE working paper, Stanford University.

Dewatripont, M. and G. Roland (1995) "Transition as a Large Scale System Change," presented at a symposium on economic history in the Econometric Society, Seventh World Congress, Tokyo.

Dinç, S. (1995) "Integration of Financial Systems and Institutional Path Dependence," mimeo, Stanford University.

Field, A. (1981) "The Problem with Neoclassical Institutional Economics: A Critique with Special Reference to the North-Thomas Model of Pre-1500 Europe," *Explorations in Economic History*, Vol. 18, pp. 174–98.

Freeman, R. (1995) "The Welfare State as a System," *American Economic Review*, Vol. 85, pp. 16–21.

Greif, A. (1994) "Cultural Beliefs and the Organization of Society: A Historical and Theoretical Reflection on Collectivist and Individualist Societies," *Journal of Political Economy*, Vol. 102, pp. 912–50.

—— (1995) "Micro Theory and the Study of Economic Institutions through Economic History: Reflections on Recent Development," presented at a symposium on economic history in the Econometric Society, Seventh World Congress, Tokyo.

Grossman, S. and O. Hart (1986) "The Costs and Benefits of Ownership: A Theory of Vertical and Lateral Integration," *Journal of Political Economy*, Vol. 94, pp. 691–719.

Holmstrom, B. (1992) "Moral Hazard in Teams," *Bell Journal of Economics*, Vol. 13, pp. 324–40.

—— and P. Milgrom (1990) "Regulating Trade Among Agents," *Journal of Institutional and Theoretical Economics*, Vol. 146, pp. 324–40.

Hurwicz, L. (1993) "Toward a Framework for Analysing Institutions and Institutional Change," in S. Bowles, H. Gintis and B. Gustafsson, eds., *Markets and Democracy*, Cambridge: Cambridge University Press, pp. 51–67.

Itoh, H. (1992) "Cooperation in Hierarchical Organizations: An Incentive Perspective," *Journal of Law, Economics and Organization*, Vol. 8, pp. 321–45.

Jian, Q. (1995) "Some Thoughts on Reforming the Management System of State-owned Assets," mimeo, Beijing.

Kandori, M. (1992) "Social Norms and Community Enforcement," *Review of Economic Studies*, Vol. 59, pp. 63–80.

Kandori, M., G. Mailath and R. Rob (1993) "Learning, Mutation, and Long Run Equilibria in Games," *Econometrica*, Vol. 16, pp. 29–56.

Krugman, P. and Obstfeld (1994) *International Economics: Theory and Policy*, third edition, New York: Harper Collins College Publisher.

McMillan, J. (1995) "Markets in Transition," presented at a symposium on transition in the Econometric Society, Seventh World Congress, Tokyo.

Matsui, A. and M. Okuno-Fujiwara (1994) "Evolution and Interaction of Cultures," mimeo, Universities of Pennsylvania and Tokyo.

Melumad, N., D. Mookherjee and S. Reichelstein (1991) "Hierarchical Decentralization of Incentive Contracts," mimeo, Stanford University.

Milgrom, P., D. North and B. Weingast (1990) "The Role of Institutions in the Revival of Trade: The Law Merchant, Private Judges, and the Champagne Fairs," *Economics and Politics*, Vol. 2, pp. 1–23.

Myerson, R. (1979) "Incentive Compatibility and the Bargaining Problem," *Econometrica*, Vol. 47, pp. 61–74.

Nelson, R. (1995) "Recent Evolutionary Theorizing about Economic Change," *Journal of Economic Literature*, Vol. 33, pp. 48–90.

Noguchi, Y. (1995) *1940 nen Taisei* (1940s Regime), Tokyo: Toyo Keizai Shinpo-sha.

North, D. (1990) *Institutions: Institutional Change and Economic Performance*, Cambridge: Cambridge University Press.

Okazaki, T. (1987) "Senji Keikau Keizai to Kakaku Tosei" (Wartime Planning Economy and Price Control), *Kindai Nihon Kenkyu*, Vol. 9, pp. 175–98.

—— and M. Okuno-Fujiwara (1994) *Gendai Nihon Keizai Sisutemu no Genryu* (The Origin of the Contemporary Japanese Economic System), Tokyo: Toyo Keizai Shinpo-sha.

Qian, Y. and C. Xu (1993) "Why China's Economic Reforms Differ: The N-Form Hierarchy and Entry/Expansion of the Non-State Sector," *Journal of Economic Transition*, Vol. 1, pp. 135–70.

Saxenian, A. (1994) *Regional Advantage*, Cambridge, Mass.: Harvard University Press.

Schotter, A. (1981) *The Economic Theory of Social Institutions*, Cambridge: Cambridge University Press.

Sugden, R. (1989) "Spontaneous Order," *Journal of Economic Perspectives*, Vol. 3, pp. 85–97.

Varian, H. (1990) "Monitoring Agents with other Agents," *Journal of Institutional and Theoretical Economics*, Vol. 146, pp. 153–74.

Wade, R. (1990) *Governing the Market: Economic Theory and the Role of the Government in East Asian Industrialization*, Princeton: Princeton University Press.

Young, H. P. (1994) "The Evolution of Conventions," *Econometrica*, Vol. 61, pp. 85–97.

Index